IN DEEP WATER

THE MARITIME ART OF ROBERT G. LLOYD

Published by:
Ferry Publications, PO Box 33, Ramsey, Isle of Man IM99 4LP
Tel: +44 (0) 1624 898445   Fax: +44 (0) 1624 898449
E-mail: ferrypubs@manx.net   Website: www.ferrypubs.co.uk

Ferry
Publications

Produced and Designed by Ferry Publications, trading as Lily Publications Ltd

Printed and bound by 1010 Printing, China

In memory of three great friends and unwavering supporters: John Maxtone-Graham, Charlie Howland and Dick Faber, alongside and 'finished with engines' – but never forgotten.

This book is dedicated to Victoria and my daughters Emilia and Lily.

Email: Robert-lloyd@btconnect.com/Website: www.robertglloyd.com

CONTENTS

FOREWORD

BY CAPTAIN KEVIN OPREY

It is with immense pride that I can recount that the pinnacle of my career was being in command of the iconic ocean liner *Queen Mary 2*. In my six years as her Master I was fortunate to be involved in a considerable number of prestigious events, one of the most significant of which was Cunard's 175th Anniversary celebrations. An event which not only allowed me to participate in celebrating a significant milestone in Cunard's history, but also to be introduced to the renowned marine artist Robert Lloyd, who was onboard to complete a painting commissioned by Cunard to mark the anniversary.

During the anniversary's special westbound Atlantic crossing, my wife mentioned that Robert was in the ship's Grand Lobby, working on his painting; intrigued by the prospect of seeing Robert at work, I made my way through the ship. As I approached Robert, my eyes were immediately drawn to the canvas where an incredibly accurate and colourful image of *Queen Mary 2* was nearing completion.

Introducing myself to Robert, we spent a considerable amount of time discussing his work and it became clear during our conversation, and others that followed, that we both had a similar passion for ships and the sea and in writing this foreword I have taken great delight in discovering other small similarities in how our shared fascination has developed.

Robert and I both grew up in great maritime cities, Robert near Liverpool, close to the River Mersey and myself in Southampton close to the Solent and Southampton Water. My childhood took place in the 50's in the days when the last of the great ocean liners struggled to compete with the introduction of commercial jet airliners. In those days, every ship from the largest ocean liner to smallest rusty old coaster captured my imagination and spending time on or close to Southampton Water I delighted in seeing ships as grand as the RMS Queen Mary, SS France, the SS United States and my favourite the RMS Caronia (all of which having featured in Robert's works). Coming from a seafaring family I was soon able to recognise the various ships from a distance by their lines and livery; it was evident my course was set for me, I was destined to spend a life at sea.

Some 20 years later, Robert took a different course. Growing up on the Wirral Peninsular close to the River Mersey, Robert could often catch a glimpse of ships from his bedroom window as they passed the 'Bar' Light Ship at the entrance to the river. Taking family walks along the New Brighton promenade, Robert would see ships making their way in and out of Liverpool docks. This being the late 70's and early 80's, many of the great liners had retired from service, however modern commercial shipping was in its evolution and Robert's interest in the sea developed on seeing the large ACL container ships, tankers and coasters that passed and from trips across the Mersey on the famed Mersey Ferries. Although I understand Robert considered a career at sea, his artistic talents led him to pursue a career in art and so after leaving school he attended Art College.

QUEEN MARY 2 ACROSS THE BOW

40x30 inches. Oil on canvas. Courtesy C. Thatcher. Private collection

QUEEN MARY 2 PASSING OSBOURNE HOUSE,

Cowes Week 2014,
30x40 inches.
Oil on canvas.
Private collection.

Robert tells me that his most enjoyable days on the Mersey Ferries were the rough days when he would remain a lone figure on a wet and windy deck whilst all others ran for shelter! Conditions that many a fair-weather passenger might consider to be the worst of a voyage are, to those of us of a certain character, the most interesting. My most exciting and enjoyable days at sea were those spent on the bridge of *Queen Mary 2*, as we forged our way across the Atlantic in a force 10 storm. Therefore, it comes as no surprise that Robert's most enjoyable days on QM2 were also the days of the crossing when conditions were at their very worst, those are the days you remember the most as they are the days that ships of QM2's stature were designed and built for.

Speaking of *Queen Mary 2*, this magnificent ship has featured in several of Robert's works. For those who have not sailed on her, QM2 across the bow and QM2 Boat Deck prom high offer a glimpse of what it is like to be 'at sea' aboard such a fine ship, whilst works like QM2 passing Osborne House offer a fellow mariners view and *Queen Mary 2* Remastered records her 2016 refit. I understand that, for Robert, Three Queens at Southampton, holds particular poignance being the painting Robert understandably records as 'closest to being a favourite'.

As you will come to recognise, Robert has not only found inspiration in the 'Cunard Queens' but also in many of the great liners, including RMS *Mauretania*

CUNARD 175

A painting completed on board the **Queen Mary 2** *during her 175th Anniversary transatlantic crossing. The painting shows the* **Queen Mary 2** *at Halifax Nova Scotia set against the background of an Admiralty Chart from 1840.*
30x30 inches.
Oil on canvas.
Courtesy Cunard Line

HMS QUEEN ELIZABETH AT ANCHOR NEW YORK HARBOUR

October 2018. 20x30 inches. Oil on canvas. Courtesy J. McGall

(in Mauretania in Moonlight), SS *United States* (in United States an American Icon), SS *Normandie* (in Normandie NY) and the SS *France* in a number of works. Beyond this, Roberts interest has turned to remarkable vessels like the elegant but ill-fated MS *Andrea Doria* (in Andrea Doria off Sardinia), and more modern ships such as the *Costa Atlantic* (in Costa Atlantic). As well as liners, cruise and passenger ships Robert has produced works of fantastic variety featuring everything from classic, historic and modern merchant ships, Naval vessels to yachts and sail boats. And Robert has also successfully turned his hand to capture the complexities of the offshore industry, shipbuilding and its associated architecture.

With such regard for his works a natural consequence of his mastery of his subject, Robert has established himself among the premier maritime painters of our time. Robert's work has been commissioned by many shipping companies and international organisations and his work can be found worldwide in numerous museum, private and Royal collections. In over twenty years painting, Robert has been recognised not only by peers, collectors and appreciators, and in the immortalisation of his works in an honorary postal stamp set, but also by Her Majesty Queen Elizabeth II.

Whilst many an artist will lean on licence, Robert's works are not only fascinating for their technical accuracy, but for also for how true to life they portray their subject,

SS. UNITED STATES CONDUCTING SPEED TRIALS

20x40 inches Oil on canvas. Private Collection

from the number of lifeboats to the curve of a hull down to the balcony rail placement. It will become apparent to you as you immerse yourself in the pages that follow that the effect is made even more impressive through the deft manner in which the light, sea conditions and skyscape are so painstakingly and effectively portrayed. Whether the product of those days on the deck of the Mersey Ferries, or just a keen eye, such is the degree of realism that you can almost feel the wind and spray on your face as the impressive vessel in front of you cuts through the waves. It is this attention to detail that makes Robert's works even more compelling.

I am sure you will discover this for yourself in this excellent collection of Robert's

works, I do so with a final thought. Great ships have a limited life sailing the world's oceans, resigned to be remembered only by the generation that witnesses their service. A talented artist bridges the historic and the current, and through their work, offer resurrection and sustainment. Ships that might otherwise have been slowly lost to time and memory are now immortalised in pencil and paint. Be it through the eyes of our children and grandchildren, or those that come after, these great ships are once again the subject of the same marvel and wonder that enthralled us as mariners, passengers and bystanders all those years before, their brilliance never to be lost. For that we can share thanks.

INTRODUCTION

According to the International Chamber of Shipping...

'The international shipping industry is responsible for the carriage of round 90% of world trade. Shipping is the life blood of the global economy. Without shipping, intercontinental trade, the bulk transport of raw materials, and the import/export of affordable food and manufactured goods would simply not be possible'.

'There are over 50,000 merchant ships trading internationally, transporting every kind of cargo. The world fleet is registered in over 150 nations and manned by over a million seafarers of virtually every nationality'.

'Ships are technically sophisticated, high value assets, larger hi-tech vessels can cost over 200 million US Dollars to build and the operation of merchant ships generates an estimated annual income of over half a trillion US Dollars in freight rates'.

… and that's just cargo ships.

The fastest growing section of shipping is undoubtedly the cruise industry, certainly it is the fastest growing category in the leisure travel industry. In 2018, a record 27.2 million passengers took a cruise and worldwide generated over 126 billion dollars, employed over 1 million people paying 41 billion dollars in wages and salaries. The cruise ship order book from 2019-2025 includes fifty new ocean going vessels representing an investment in excess of 51 billion dollars.

None of the above takes into account ferries, offshore and specialist vessels There are a lot of ships (and sea) to paint!

Marine Art – definition:

Marine art or maritime art is any form of figurative art (that is, painting, drawing, printmaking and sculpture) that portrays or draws its main inspiration from the sea. Maritime painting is a genre that depicts ships and the sea—a genre particularly strong from the 17th to 19th centuries. In practice the term often covers art showing shipping on rivers and estuaries, beach scenes and all art showing boats, without any rigid distinction - for practical reasons subjects that can be drawn or painted from dry land in fact feature strongly in the genre. Strictly speaking "maritime art" should always include some element of human seafaring, whereas "marine art" would also include pure seascapes with no human element, though this distinction may not be observed in practice.

Ships and boats have been included in art from almost the earliest times, but marine art only began to become a distinct genre, with specialised artists, towards the end of the Middle Ages, mostly in the form of the "ship portrait" a type of work that is still popular and concentrates on depicting a single vessel.

Robert Lloyd works on a giant mural for the American Bureau of Shipping

When I first starting painting many of the companies I worked for and the ships I painted were British, how times have changed. In twenty-five years just about all of those companies have disappeared to be swallowed up by larger and arguably more progressive and forward-thinking organisations. It is with great sadness that no 'British Ships' of the modern era are represented here apart from an Isle of Wight Ferry. Even the great Cunarder's are now registered overseas, times are changing, you could argue times HAVE changed and we will never again be the great ship building and ship owning island nation we once were.

Every painting in this book has some sea or at least water apart from probably the most important painting of all, at least from a personal perspective, in the acknowledgements. I love painting the sea, I love painting the sky and one might argue, ships just happen to be there! I hope you enjoy the images, I hope to do many more.

Robert G. Lloyd. England
June 2019.

GOELO AND VIKING VENTURER

Passing each other off the Isle of Wight. 20x30 inches oil on canvas board. Courtesy Miles Cowsill

THE GREAT OCEAN LINERS

An ocean liner is a passenger ship primarily used as a form of transportation across seas or oceans. Liners may also carry cargo or mail and often operate over set routes according to established schedules.

Ocean liners are usually strongly built with a high freeboard to withstand rough seas and adverse conditions encountered in the open ocean. Additionally, they are often designed with thicker hull plating than is found on cruise ships, and have large capacities for fuel, food and other consumables on long voyages.

The first ocean liners were built in the mid-19th century. Technological innovations such as the steam engine and steel hull allowed larger and faster liners to be built, giving rise to a competition between world powers of the time, especially between the United Kingdom and Germany. Once the dominant form of travel between continents, ocean liners were rendered largely obsolete by the emergence of long-distance aircraft after World War II. Advances in automobile and railway technology also played a role. By 2015, the only ship still in service as an ocean liner is the RMS *Queen Mary 2* after RMS *Queen Elizabeth 2* was retired in 2008. Of the many ships constructed over the decades, only nine ocean liners made before 1967 survive.

Ocean liners were the primary mode of intercontinental travel for over a century, from the mid-19th century until they began to be supplanted by airliners in the 1950s. In addition to passengers, liners carried mail and cargo. Ships contracted to carry British Royal Mail used the designation RMS. Liners were also the preferred way to move gold and other high value cargoes.

The busiest route for liners was on the North Atlantic with ships travelling between Europe and North America. It was on this route that the fastest, largest and most advanced liners travelled. But while in contemporary popular imagination the term "ocean liners" evokes these transatlantic superliners, most ocean liners historically were mid-sized vessels which served as the common carriers of passengers and freight between nations and among mother countries and their colonies and dependencies in the pre-jet age. Such routes included Europe to African and Asian colonies, Europe to South America, and migrant traffic from Europe to North America in the 19th and first two decades of the 20th centuries, and to Canada and Australia after the Second World War.

Beginning at the advent of the Jet Age, where transoceanic ship service declined, a gradual transition from passenger ships as mean of transportation to nowadays cruise ships started. In order for ocean liners to remain profitable, cruise lines have modified some of them to operate on cruise routes, such as *Queen Elizabeth 2* and SS *France*. Certain characteristics of older ocean liners made them unsuitable for cruising, such as high fuel consumption, deep draught preventing them from entering shallow ports, and cabins designed to maximise passenger numbers rather than comfort.

The Italian Line's SS *Michelangelo* and SS *Raffaello*, the last ocean liners to be built primarily for crossing the North Atlantic, could not be converted economically and had short careers.

*Preparatory pencil sketch of RMS **Lusitania** leaving her builders on the River Clyde*

The most important of all routes taken by ocean liners was the North Atlantic route which accounted for a large part of the clientele, who travelled between ports of Liverpool, Southampton, Hamburg, Le Havre, Cherbourg, Cobh, and New York City. The profitability of this route came from migration to the United States. The need for speed influenced the construction of liners for this route, and the Blue Riband was awarded to the liner with the highest speed. The route was not without danger, as storms and icebergs were common in the North Atlantic. Many shipwrecks occurred on this route, the most famous of which was that of RMS *Titanic* and the *Andrea Doria*. This route was the preferred route for major shipping companies and was the scene of fierce competition between them.

RMS *Titanic* was a British passenger liner that sank in the North Atlantic Ocean in 1912, after colliding with an iceberg during her maiden voyage from Southampton to New York City. Of the estimated 2,224 passengers and crew aboard, more than 1,500 died, making it one of modern history's deadliest commercial marine disasters during peacetime. RMS *Titanic* was the largest ship afloat at the time she entered service and was the second of three Olympic-class ocean liners operated by the White Star Line. She was built by the Harland and Wolff shipyard in Belfast. Thomas Andrews, chief naval architect of the shipyard at the time, died in the disaster.

NEW YORK CIRCA 1957.

35x45 inches. Oil on canvas. Private collection

RMS *Titanic* was under the command of Capt. Edward Smith, who also went down with the ship. The ocean liner carried some of the wealthiest people in the world, as well as hundreds of emigrants from Great Britain and Ireland, Scandinavia and elsewhere throughout Europe who were seeking a new life in the United States. The first class accommodation was designed to be the pinnacle of comfort and luxury, with an on board gymnasium, swimming pool, libraries, high-class restaurants and opulent cabins. A high-powered radiotelegraph transmitter was available for sending passenger "marconigrams" and for the ship's operational use. Although *Titanic* had advanced safety features such as watertight compartments and remotely activated watertight doors, it only carried enough lifeboats for 1,178 people – about half the

11

SS TITANIC

Pictured at 1.30 am on the 15th April 1912. 25x35 inches. Oil on canvas. Private collection

RMS LUSITANIA
Pictured on her maiden arrival at Liverpool. 25x35 inches. Oil on canvas. Private collection

SS. LIBERTÉ
Early evening Eastbound Atlantic. 25x35 inches. Oil on canvas. Courtesy Jack Fahy

number on board, and one-third of her total capacity—due to outdated maritime safety regulations. The ship carried 16 lifeboat davits which could lower three lifeboats each, for a total of forty-eight boats. However, *Titanic* carried only a total of twenty lifeboats, four of which were collapsible and proved hard to launch during the sinking.

After leaving Southampton on 10 April 1912, she called at Cherbourg in France and Queenstown (now Cobh) in Ireland before heading west to New York. On 14 April, four days into the crossing and about 375 miles (600 km) south of Newfoundland, she hit an iceberg at 11:40 p.m. ship's time. The collision caused the hull plates to buckle inwards along her starboard (right) side and opened five of her sixteen watertight compartments to the sea; she could only survive four flooding. Meanwhile, passengers and some crew members were evacuated in lifeboats, many of which were launched only partially loaded. A disproportionate number of men were left aboard because of a "women and children first" protocol for loading lifeboats. At 2:20 a.m., she broke apart and foundered with well over one thousand people still aboard. Just under two hours after Titanic sank, the Cunard liner RMS *Carpathia* arrived and brought aboard an estimated 705 survivors.

RMS *Lusitania* and her sister the *Mauretania* were commissioned by Cunard, responding to increasing competition from rival transatlantic passenger companies, particularly the German Norddeutscher Lloyd (NDL) and Hamburg America Line (HAPAG). They had larger, faster, more modern and more luxurious ships than Cunard, and were better placed, starting from German ports, to capture the lucrative trade in emigrants leaving Europe for North America. The NDL liner *Kaiser Wilhelm der Grosse* captured the Blue Riband from Cunard's Campania in 1897, before the prize was taken in 1900 by the HAPAG ship *Deutschland*. NDL soon wrested the prize back in 1903 with the new *Kaiser Wilhelm II* and *Kronprinz Wilhelm*. Cunard saw its passenger numbers affected as a result of the so-called "Kaiser-class ocean liners".

American millionaire businessman J. P. Morgan had decided to invest in transatlantic shipping by creating a new company, International Mercantile Marine (IMM), and, in 1901, purchased the British freight shipper Frederick Leyland & Co. and a controlling interest in the British passenger White Star Line and folded them into IMM. In 1902, IMM, NDL and HAPAG entered into a "Community of Interest" to fix prices and divide among them the transatlantic trade. The partners also acquired a 51% stake in the Dutch Holland America Line. IMM made offers to purchase Cunard which, along with the French CGT, was now its principal rival.

Cunard chairman Lord Inverclyde thus approached the British government for assistance. Faced with the impending collapse of the British liner fleet and the consequent loss of national prestige, as well as the reserve of shipping for war purposes which it represented, they agreed to help. By an agreement signed in June 1903, Cunard was given a loan of £2.6 million to finance two ships, repayable over 20 years at a favourable interest rate of 2.75%. The ships would receive an annual operating subsidy of £75,000 each plus a mail contract worth £68,000. In return, the ships would be built to Admiralty specifications so that they could be used as auxiliary cruisers in wartime

RMS *Lusitania* was a holder of the Blue Riband appellation for the fastest Atlantic crossing and was briefly the world's largest passenger ship until the completion of her sister ship *Mauretania*, three months later. The Cunard Line launched *Lusitania* in 1906, at a time of fierce competition for the North Atlantic trade. She sank on her 202nd transatlantic crossing.

Both *Lusitania* and *Mauretania* were fitted with revolutionary new turbine engines

that enabled them to maintain a service speed of twenty-five knots (46 km/h; 29 mph). They were equipped with lifts, wireless telegraph and electric light, and provided 50% more passenger space than any other ship; the first class decks were noted for their sumptuous furnishings.

The Royal Navy had blockaded Germany at the start of the First World War. The UK declared the entire North Sea a war zone in the autumn of 1914 and mined the approaches; in the spring of 1915 all food imports for Germany were declared contraband. When RMS *Lusitania* left New York for Britain on 1 May 1915, German submarine warfare was intensifying in the Atlantic. Germany had declared the seas around the United Kingdom a war zone, and the German embassy in the United States had placed newspaper advertisements warning people of the dangers of sailing on *Lusitania*.

On the afternoon of 7 May, a German U-boat torpedoed the *Lusitania* eleven mi (18 km) off the southern coast of Ireland and inside the declared war zone. A second, unexplained, internal explosion, probably that of munitions she was carrying, sent her to the seabed in 18 minutes, with the deaths of 1,198 passengers and crew.

When the Imperial German Navy sank, without warning, what was a completely defenceless, officially non-military ship, killing almost a thousand civilians, many of whom were children, the Germans were accused of breaching the internationally recognised Cruiser Rules. With the British introduction of Q-ships in 1915 with concealed deck guns, it had become more dangerous for submarines to give warning. (Lusitania had been fitted with 6-inch gun mounts in 1913, although no guns were mounted at the time of her sinking.)

The sinking caused a storm of protest in the United States because 128 American citizens were among the dead. The sinking helped shift public opinion in the United States against Germany and was a factor in the United States' declaration of war nearly two years later. After the First World War, successive British governments maintained that there were no munitions on board *Lusitania,* and the Germans were not justified in treating the ship as a naval vessel. In 1982, the head of the British Foreign Office's North America department finally admitted that there is a large amount of ammunition in the wreck, some of which is highly dangerous and poses a safety risk to salvage teams.

SS *Andrea Doria*, was an ocean liner for the Italian Line (Società di navigazione Italia) home ported in Genoa, Italy, most famous for her sinking in 1956, when forty-six people were killed.

Named after the 16th-century Genoese admiral Andrea Doria, the ship had a gross register tonnage of 29,100 and a capacity of about 1,200 passengers and 500 crew. For a country attempting to rebuild its economy and reputation after World War II, *Andrea Doria* was an icon of Italian national pride. Of all Italy's ships at the time, *Andrea Doria* was the largest, fastest, and supposedly safest. Launched on 16 June 1951, the ship undertook its maiden voyage on 14 January 1953.

On 25 July 1956, while *Andrea Doria* was approaching the coast of Nantucket, Massachusetts, bound for New York City, the eastbound MS *Stockholm* of the Swedish American Line collided with it in one of history's most infamous maritime disasters. Struck in the side, the top-heavy *Andrea Doria* immediately started to list severely to starboard, which left half of its lifeboats unusable. The consequent shortage of lifeboats could have resulted in significant loss of life, but the efficiency of the ship's technical design allowed it to stay afloat for over 11 hours after the ramming. The good behaviour of the crew, improvements in communications, and the rapid response of other ships averted a disaster similar in scale to that of *Titanic* in 1912. While 1,660

SS. EMPRESS OF BRITAIN PICTURED AT NIGHT

20x30 inches. Oil on canvas. Courtesy Frank Trumbour

Preparatory sketch for RMS **Queen Elizabeth**

Preparatory sketch for **Michelangelo** *arriving at New York*

passengers and crew were rescued and survived, forty-six people died with the ship as a consequence of the collision. The evacuated luxury liner capsized and sank the following morning. This accident remains the worst maritime disaster to occur in United States waters since the sinking of the SS *Eastland* in 1915.

The incident and its aftermath were heavily covered by the news media. While the rescue efforts were both successful and commendable, the cause of the collision with Stockholm and the loss of Andrea Doria generated much interest in the media and many lawsuits. Largely because of an out-of-court settlement agreement between the two shipping companies during hearings immediately after the disaster, no determination of the cause(s) was ever formally published. Although greater blame appeared initially to fall on the Italian liner, more recent discoveries have indicated that a misreading of radar on the Swedish ship initiated the collision course, leading to errors on both ships

SS *Michelangelo* was an Italian ocean liner built in 1965 for Italian Line by Ansaldo Shipyards, Genoa. She was one of the last ships to be built primarily for liner service across the North Atlantic. Her sister ship was the SS *Raffaello*.

As Italy's flagship SS *Michelangelo* made her last Atlantic crossing in July 1975, under command of Senior Captain Claudio Cosulich. Afterwards she was laid up at La Spezia alongside her sister. Several buyers (including Knut Kloster of Norwegian Cruise Line) inspected the ships but did not wish to buy them due to the costs required to modernise them to cruise ship standard. There was one serious buyer, Home Lines, who wished to buy the ships and keep them under Italian flag for cruising in the Caribbean. The Italian Line refused to sell the sisters, reportedly because they felt keeping the Italian flag would have associated the "embarrassing money-losers" with them.

In 1976 a buyer was found that agreed to the terms sought by Italian Line. The Shah of Iran purchased the ships, to be used as floating barracks. The ships that had cost $45 million each were now sold at the price of $2 million per ship. The *Michelangelo* ended up in Bandar Abbas where she was to spend the next fifteen years.

In 1978 plans were made to reconstruct her as the luxury cruise ship *Scià Reza il Grande* (in honour of Rez Shah). However, an expert inspection team sent from Italy came to the conclusion she was too badly deteriorated to make rebuilding a viable option. Similar plans were made again in 1983, but they too fell short. Finally, in June 1991, an end was put to the *Michelangelo's* suffering when she was scrapped in Pakistan.

The SS *Constitution* was an ocean liner owned by American Export Lines. Commissioned in 1951, she started her long career sailing on the New York City-Genoa-Naples-Gibraltar route to Europe. Constitution was a sister ship to the SS *Independence*. SS *Constitution* was featured in several episodes of the situation comedy I Love Lucy starring Lucille Ball and Desi Arnaz, starting with episode, "Bon Voyage," aired January 16, 1956. Lucy Ricardo missed the ship and had to be ferried by air by a then-novel helicopter.

American movie actress Grace Kelly sailed aboard SS *Constitution* from New York to Monaco for her wedding to Prince Rainier in 1956.

SS *Constitution* was featured in the 1957 film, An Affair to Remember starring Cary Grant and Deborah Kerr. Former President Harry S. Truman and his wife Bess sailed back to New York from Europe on the *Constitution* in the summer of 1958. The ship was also featured in the beginning and end of an episode of the Naked City TV series titled "No Naked Ladies in Front of Giovanni's House!" aired April 17, 1963. The ship also featured prominently in the Magnum, P.I. television series episode titled "All Thieves on Deck" aired January 30, 1986.

Following service on American Export's "Sunlane" cruise to Europe in the 1950s and 1960s the two ships sailed for American Hawaii Cruises for many years in the 1980s and 1990s; as US ships with US crews meeting the criteria of the Passenger Services Act they were able to cruise the Islands without sailing to a foreign port.

SS *Constitution* was retired in 1995; while under tow to be scrapped, she sank some 700 nautical miles (1,300 km) north of the Hawaiian Islands on November 17, 1997.

The SS Normandie was an ocean liner built in Saint-Nazaire, (cont on page 29)
(from page 17) France, for the French Line Compagnie Générale Transatlantique

SS ANDREA DORIA

pictured in the Straits of Gibraltar heading into the Atlantic swells. 25x35 inches. Oil on canvas. Courtesy Jack Fahy

SS ANDREA DORIA

in the Bay of Naples, 25x35 inches. Oil on canvas. Courtesy Vincent Amabile

SS. REX PICTURED IN THE BAY OF NAPLES

25x35 inches. Oil on canvas. Courtesy Vincent Amabile

SS. MICHELANGELO
Pictured arriving in New York. 25x35 inches. Oil on canvas. Curtesy Vincent Amabile

SS CONSTITUTION

In the Bay of Naples. 25x35 inches. Oil on canvas. Courtesy Jack Fahy

SS NORMANDIE

Pictured at anchor in New York Harbour. 20x30 inches. Oil on canvas. Courtesy Jack Fahy

SS FRANCE AT NEW YORK

30x40 inches. Courtesy Miles Cowsill

SS FRANCE EARLY MORNING ARRIVAL AT NEW YORK

20x30 inches. Oil on canvas. Courtesy Jack Fahy

SS. CONSTITUTION AT SEA

20x30 inches. Oil on canvas. Courtesy Frank Trumbour

RMS MAURETANIA II

Pictured at Cobh. 25x35 inches. Oil on canvas. Private collection

A RACE TO THE FINISH

SS **United States** *approaching New York with the RMS* **Queen Mary***. 20x30 inches oil on canvas. Private Collection*

SS UNITED STATES PASSING RMS QUEEN MARY

In the Solent. 20x30 inches. Oil on canvas. Artist's collection

*Preliminary sketch layout of the SS **United States** leaving New York*

(CGT). She entered service in 1935 as the largest and fastest passenger ship afloat; she remains the most powerful steam turbo-electric-propelled passenger ship ever built.

Her novel design and lavish interiors led many to consider her the greatest of ocean liners. Despite this, she was not a commercial success and relied partly on government subsidy to operate. During service as the flagship of the CGT, she made 139 westbound transatlantic crossings from her home port of Le Havre to New York. *Normandie* held the Blue Riband for the fastest transatlantic crossing at several points during her service career, during which the RMS *Queen Mary* was her main rival.

During World War II, *Normandie* was seized by US authorities at New York and renamed USS *Lafayette*. In 1942, the liner caught fire while being converted to a troopship, capsized onto her port side and came to rest on the mud of the Hudson River at Pier 88, the site of the current New York Passenger Ship Terminal. Although salvaged at great expense, restoration was deemed too costly and she was scrapped in October 1946

SS *France* was a Compagnie Générale Transatlantique (CGT, or French Line) ocean liner, constructed by the Chantiers de l'Atlantique shipyard at Saint-Nazaire, France, and put into service in February 1962. At the time of her construction in 1960, the 316 m (1,037 ft) vessel was the longest passenger ship ever built, a record that remained unchallenged until the construction of the 345 m (1,132 ft) RMS *Queen*

Two preliminary sketches of **Queen Elizabeth 2**

Mary 2 in 2004. France was constructed to replace the line's other ageing ships like SS *Ile de France* and SS *Liberté,* which were outdated by the 1950s. Without these vessels the French Line had no ability to compete against their rivals, most notably the Cunard Line, which also had plans for constructing a new modern liner. It was rumoured that this ship would be a 75,000-ton replacement for their ships RMS *Queen Mary* and RMS *Queen Elizabeth*. At this time the United States Lines had put into service in 1952 SS *United States*, which had broken all speed records on her maiden voyage, with an average speed of 35.59 knots (65.91 km/h; 40.96 mph).

The *France* was later purchased by Norwegian Cruise Line (NCL) in 1979, renamed SS *Norway* and underwent significant modifications that better suited her for cruising duties. She was renamed SS *Blue Lady* and sold to be scrapped in 2006, and scrapping was completed in late 2008.

SS *United States* was built in 1950–51 for the United States Lines at a cost of US$79.4 million. The ship is the largest ocean liner constructed entirely in the United States and the fastest ocean liner to cross the Atlantic in either direction, retaining the Blue Riband for the highest average speed since her maiden voyage in 1952. She was designed by American naval architect William Francis Gibbs and could be converted into a troopship if required by the Navy in time of war. The United States maintained an uninterrupted schedule of transatlantic passenger service until 1969 and was never used as a troopship.

The ship has been sold several times since the 1970s, with each new owner trying unsuccessfully to make the liner profitable. Eventually, the ship's fittings were sold at auction, and hazardous wastes, including asbestos panels throughout the ship, were removed, leaving her almost completely stripped by 1994. Two years later, she was towed to Pier eighty-two on the Delaware River, in Philadelphia, where she remains today.

Since 2009, a preservation group called the SS United States Conservancy has been raising funds to save the ship. The group purchased her in 2011 and has drawn up several unrealised plans to restore the ship, one of which included turning the ship into a multi-purpose waterfront complex.

Queen Elizabeth 2, often referred to simply as *QE2*, was built for the Cunard Line

and was operated by Cunard as both a transatlantic liner and a cruise ship from 1969 to 2008. Since 18 April 2018 she has been operating as a floating hotel in Dubai.

QE2 was designed for the transatlantic service from her home port of Southampton, UK, to New York, and was named after the earlier Cunard liner RMS *Queen Elizabeth.*

She served as the flagship of the line from 1969 until succeeded by *Queen Mary 2* in 2004. Designed in Cunard's then headquarters and regional offices in Liverpool and Southampton respectively, and built in Clydebank, Scotland, *QE2* was considered the last of the great transatlantic ocean liners until *Queen Mary 2* entered service.

The *QE2* was also the last oil fired passenger steamship to cross the Atlantic in

Preliminary sketch of **Queen Mary 2** *leaving New York*

A BROADSIDE VIEW OF QUEEN ELIZABETH 2

Pictured mid-Atlantic. 30x40 inches. Oil on canvas. Courtesy of Jack Fahy

QUEEN ELIZABETH 2 AND QUEEN MARY 2

Pictured together eastbound Transatlantic. 25x35 inches. Oil on canvas. Courtesy Christoph Walter

QUEEN ELIZABETH

Pictured at Flam, Norway. 20x16 inches. Oil on canvas. Private collection

scheduled liner service until she was refitted with a modern diesel powerplant in 1986/1987. During almost forty years of service, *Queen Elizabeth 2* undertook regular world cruises and later operated predominantly as a cruise ship, sailing out of Southampton, England. *QE2* had no running mate and never ran a year-round weekly transatlantic express service to New York. *QE2* did, however, continue the Cunard tradition of regular scheduled transatlantic crossings every year of her service life. She was never given a Royal Mail Ship designation, instead carrying the SS and later MV or MS prefixes in official documents.

She was retired from active Cunard service on 27 November 2008. She had been acquired by the private equity arm of Dubai World, which planned to begin conversion of the vessel to a 500-room floating hotel moored at the Palm Jumeirah, Dubai. The 2008 financial crisis, however, intervened and the ship was laid up at Dubai Drydocks and later Port Rashid. Subsequent conversion plans were announced by Istithmar in 2012 and by the Oceanic Group in 2013 but these both stalled. In November 2015 Cruise Arabia & Africa quoted DP World chairman Ahmed Sultan Bin Sulayem as saying that *QE2* would not be scrapped and in March 2017, a Dubai-based construction company announced it had been contracted to refurbish the ship.

The restored *QE2* opened to visitors on 18 April 2018, with a soft opening, with discounted rates and only five of the planned thirteen restaurants and bars completed. The grand opening took place in late 2018.

Queen Mary 2 is the largest ocean liner ever built, having served as the flagship of the Cunard Line since succeeding the *Queen Elizabeth 2* in 2004.

The new ship was named by Queen Elizabeth II in 2004 after the first RMS *Queen Mary* of 1936. Queen Mary was in turn named after Mary of Teck, consort of King George V. With the retirement of *Queen Elizabeth 2* in 2008, *Queen Mary 2* is the only passenger ship operating as an ocean liner – for a part of each year (as of 2019) offering a transatlantic service between Southampton, England, and New York City, United States. The ship is also used for cruising, including an annual world cruise.

She was designed by a team of British naval architects led by Dr. Stephen Payne and was constructed in France by Chantiers de l'Atlantique. At the time of her construction, *Queen Mary 2* held the distinctions of being the longest, at 1,131.99 ft (345.03 m), and largest, with a gross tonnage of 148,528 GT, passenger ship ever built. She no longer held this distinction after the construction of Royal Caribbean International's 154,407 GT *Freedom of the Seas* (a cruise ship) in April 2006 but remains the largest ocean liner ever built.

Queen Mary 2 was intended for routine crossings of the Atlantic Ocean and was therefore designed differently from many other passenger ships. The liner's final cost was approximately $300,000 US per berth. Expenses were increased by the high quality of materials, and having been designed as an ocean liner, she required 40% more steel than a standard cruise ship. *Queen Mary 2* has a maximum speed of just over 30 knots (56 km/h; 35 mph) and a cruising speed of twenty-six knots (48 km/h; 30 mph), much faster than a contemporary cruise ship. Instead of the diesel-electric configuration found on many ships, *Queen Mary 2* uses integrated electric propulsion to achieve her top speed. Diesel engines, augmented by gas turbines, are used to generate electricity for electric motors for propulsion and for on board use.

Some of *Queen Mary 2*'s facilities include fifteen restaurants and bars, five swimming pools, a casino, a ballroom, a theatre, and the first planetarium at sea.

Case Study, Cunard

In 1839 Samuel Cunard, a Halifax, Nova Scotia shipowner, was awarded the first British transatlantic steamship mail contract, and the next year formed the British and North American Royal Mail Steam Packet Company together with Robert Napier, the famous Scottish steamship engine designer and builder, to operate the line's four pioneer paddle steamers on the Liverpool-Halifax-Boston route. For most of the next 30 years, Cunard held the Blue Riband for the fastest Atlantic voyage. However, in the 1870s Cunard fell behind its rivals, the White Star Line and the Inman Line. To meet this competition, in 1879 the firm was reorganised as the Cunard Steamship Company, Ltd, to raise capital.

In 1902 White Star joined the American-owned International Mercantile Marine Co. and the British government provided Cunard with substantial loans and a subsidy to build two superliners needed to retain its competitive position. *Mauretania* held the

SS BRITANNIA *Pictured in Halifax on her maiden voyage*
30x40 inches. Oil on canvas. Courtesy John Langley

RMS **Britannia** *departing Liverpool on her maiden Voyage*

Blue Riband from 1909 to 1929. The sinking of her running mate *Lusitania* in 1915 was one of the causes of the United States' entering the First World War. In the late 1920s, Cunard faced new competition when the Germans, Italians and French built large prestige liners. Cunard was forced to suspend construction on its own new superliner because of the Great Depression. In 1934 the British government offered Cunard loans to finish *Queen Mary* and to build a second ship, *Queen Elizabeth*, on the condition that Cunard merged with the then ailing White Star Line to form Cunard White Star Ltd. Cunard owned two-thirds of the new company. Cunard purchased White Star's share in 1947; the name reverted to the Cunard Line in 1950.

Upon the end of the Second World War, Cunard regained its position as the largest Atlantic passenger line. By the mid-1950s, it operated twelve ships to the United States and Canada. After 1958, transatlantic passenger ships became increasingly unprofitable because of the introduction of jet airliners. Cunard withdrew from its year-round service in 1968 to concentrate on cruising and summer transatlantic voyages for vacationers. The Queens were replaced by *Queen Elizabeth 2*, which was designed for the dual role.

In 1998 Cunard was acquired by the Carnival Corporation and accounted for 8.7% of that company's revenue in 2012. In 2004, *QE2* was replaced on the transatlantic runs by *Queen Mary 2*. The line also operates *Queen Victoria* (QV) and *Queen Elizabeth* (QE). Now, Cunard is the only shipping company to operate a scheduled passenger service between Europe and North America.

The Britannia class was the Cunard Line's initial fleet of wooden paddlers that established the first year-round scheduled Atlantic steamship service in 1840. By 1845, steamships carried half of the transatlantic saloon passengers and Cunard dominated this trade. While the units of the Britannia class were solid performers, they were not superior to many of the other steamers being placed on the Atlantic at that time. What made the Britannia's successful is that they were the first homogeneous class of

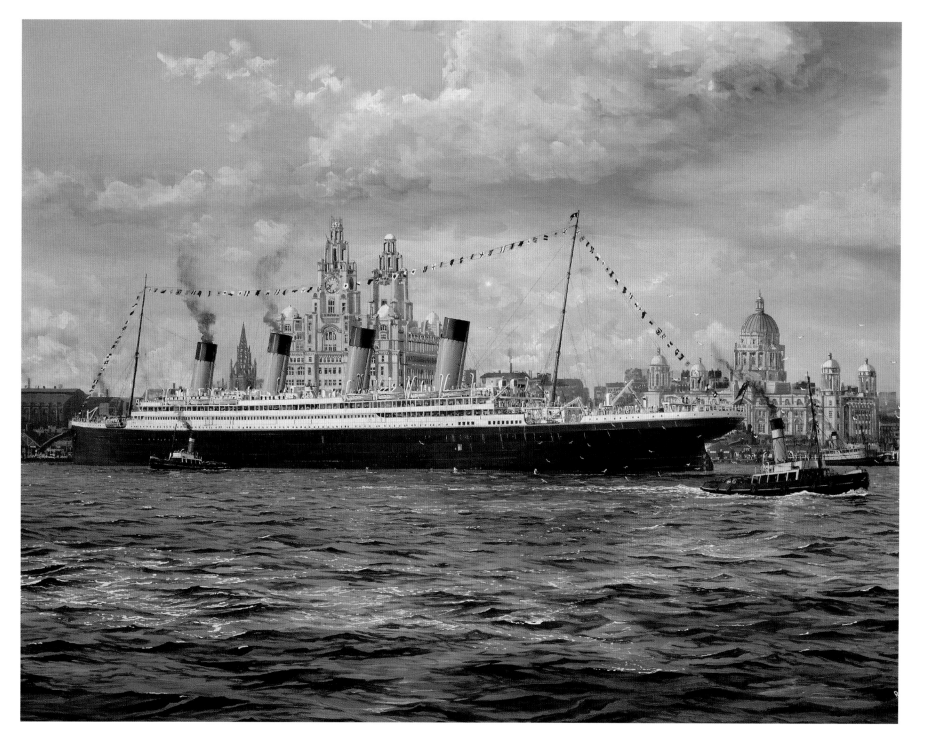

RMS OLYMPIC

Pictured arriving at Liverpool. 25x35 inches. Oil on canvas. Private collection

QUEEN ELIZABETH 2, QUEEN MARY 2 AND QUEEN VICTORIA

Pictured at Southampton. 110x60 inches. Oil on canvas. Courtesy Cunard Line

transatlantic steamships to provide a frequent and uniform service. *Britannia*, *Acadia* and *Caledonia* were commissioned in 1840 and Columbia in 1841 enabling Cunard to provide the dependable schedule of sailings required under his mail contracts with the Admiralty. It was these mail contracts that enabled Cunard to survive when all his early competitors failed.

Cunard's ships were reduced versions of *Great Western* and only carried 115 passengers in conditions that Charles Dickens unfavourably likened to a "gigantic hearse". Crossing times were scheduled at 13 days, 6 hours (7.9 knots) westbound and 11 days, 3 hours (9.3 knots) eastbound. The initial four units were insufficient to meet the contracted sailings, and an enhanced unit, the *Hibernia* was commissioned in 1843. When *Columbia* was wrecked in 1843 without loss of life, *Cambria* was ordered to replace her.

In 1849 and 1850, the surviving original units along with *Hibernia* were sold to foreign navies after completing forty round trips for Cunard. *Cambria* remained in the Cunard fleet for another decade.

In March 1849 *Britannia* was sold to the German Confederation Navy and renamed SMS *Barbarossa*. Fitted with nine guns, she served as the flagship of the Reichsflotte under Karl Rudolf Brommy in the Battle of Heligoland. In June 1852 she was transferred to the Prussian Navy and used as a barracks ship at Danzig.

Twenty-eight years later, she was decommissioned and in July 1880 she was sunk as a target ship.

RMS *Mauretania* was designed by Leonard Peskett and built by Wigham Richardson and Swan Hunter for Cunard Line, launched on the afternoon of 20 September 1906. She was the world's largest ship until the completion of RMS *Olympic* in 1911. *Mauretania* became a favourite among her passengers. She captured the Eastbound Blue Riband on her maiden return voyage in December 1907, then claimed the Westbound Blue Riband for the fastest transatlantic crossing during her 1909 season. She held both speed records for 20 years.

The ship's name was taken from the ancient Roman province of *Mauretania* on the northwest African coast, not the modern *Mauritania* to the south. Similar nomenclature was also employed by *Mauretania's* running mate *Lusitania*, which was named after the Roman province directly north of *Mauretania*, across the Strait of Gibraltar in Portugal. *Mauretania* remained in service until 1934 when Cunard White Star retired her; scrapping commenced in 1935.

The RMS *Franconia* was built for the Cunard Line and operated from 1922 to 1956. She was second of three liners named *Franconia* which served the Cunard Line, the others being RMS *Franconia* built in 1910 and the third *Franconia* in 1963.

She was launched on 21 October 1922 at the John Brown & Co shipyard in

RMS FRANCONIA
Pictured approaching Cape Race. 20x35 inches. Oil on canvas. Artist's collection

Clydebank, Scotland. Her maiden voyage was between Liverpool and New York in June 1923; she was employed on this route in the summer months until World War II. In the winter she was used on world cruises. The *Franconia* was retired in 1956 with her fleet mate RMS *Ascania* having been replaced on the Canadian run by the Saxonia, Ivernia and the *Carinthia*. She was scrapped at Inverkeithing by Thos. W. Ward, December 1956.

RMS *Mauretania* was launched on 28 July 1938 at the Cammell Laird yard in Birkenhead, England, and was completed in May 1939. The second *Mauretania* was the first ship built for the newly formed Cunard White Star company following the merger in April 1934 of the Cunard and White Star Line. On the withdrawal of the first RMS *Mauretania* in 1934, to prevent a rival company using the name and to keep it available for the new liner, arrangements were made for the Red Funnel paddle steamer Queen to be renamed *Mauretania* in the interim.

The new liner had a tonnage of 35,739 gross, an overall length of 772 feet (235 m) and a beam of 89 feet (27 m) and had an exterior design similar to RMS *Queen Elizabeth*. The vessel was powered by two sets of Parsons single reduction geared steam turbines giving 42,000 shaft horsepower (31,000 kW) and driving twin propellers. Her service speed was twenty-three knots (43 km/h) with a maximum speed of twenty-six knots (48 km/h).

By 1962, *Mauretania* was facing competition from more modern ships and was beginning to lose money for Cunard Line. In October 1962 the ship was painted pale green, like *Caronia* (the famed Green Goddess), and the passenger accommodation was adjusted to accommodate 406 First class, 364 Cabin class and 357 Tourist class passengers. On 28 March 1963 she began a new Mediterranean service calling at New York, Cannes, Genoa and Naples. This was a failure, and by 1964 she was mainly employed cruising from New York to the West Indies.

Mauretania's final voyage was a Mediterranean cruise which left New York on 15 September 1965. It was announced that on her return to Southampton, *Mauretania* would be withdrawn from service and sold. She arrived at Southampton on 10 October 1965 and had already been sold to the British Iron & Steel Corporation. Leaving Southampton on 20 November for her final voyage, she arrived at Thos W Ward's shipbreaking yard in Inverkeithing, Fife, Scotland. She was commanded by Capt. John Treasure Jones who had been Master since 1962. He navigated the mud straits of the Forth without tugboats and made the final berthing through the shallows above the mud banks on the midnight high tide. By late April 1966, her funnels were gone, and by mid-1966, the superstructure was removed, leaving only the keel of the ship. Scrapping was finished by late 1966. (cont on page 40)

LUXURY LINER ROW, NEW YORK SUMMER 1953

30x40 inches. Oil on canvas. Courtesy Jack Fahy

RMS QUEEN ELIZABETH

Pictured on the River Clyde. 30x40 inches. Oil on canvas. Courtesy Jack Fahy

QUEEN MARY 2
Pictured approaching Cape Town. 30x40 inches. Private collection.

(from page 37)   The RMS *Queen Elizabeth* was built by John Brown and Company and was designed to be an improvement upon the design of RMS *Queen Mary* with sufficient changes, including a reduction in the number of boilers to twelve instead of *Queen Mary's* twenty-four, that the designers could discard one funnel and increase deck, cargo and passenger space. The two funnels were self-supporting and braced internally to give a cleaner looking appearance. With the forward well deck omitted, a more refined hull shape was achieved, and a sharper, raked bow was added for a third bow-anchor point. She was to be eleven feet longer and of 4,000 tons greater displacement than her older sister ship, *Queen Mary*. With *Queen Mary* she provided weekly luxury liner service between Southampton in the United Kingdom and New York City in the United States, via Cherbourg in France.

While being constructed in the mid-1930s by John Brown and Company at Clydebank, Scotland, the build was known as Hull 552. Launched on 27 September 1938, she was named in honour of Queen Elizabeth, then Queen Consort to King George VI, who became the Queen Mother in 1952. She was the largest passenger liner ever built at that time and for 56 years thereafter. She also has the distinction of being the largest-ever riveted ship by gross tonnage. She first entered service in February 1940 as a troopship in World War II, and it was not until October 1946 that she served in her intended role as an ocean liner.

With the decline in the popularity of the transatlantic route, both ships were replaced by the smaller, more economical *Queen Elizabeth 2* in 1969. *Queen Mary* was retired from service on 9 December 1967, and was sold to the city of Long Beach, California. *Queen Elizabeth* was sold to a succession of buyers, most of whom had unsuccessful plans for her. Finally, *Queen Elizabeth* was sold to Hong Kong businessman Tung Chao Yung, who intended to convert her into a floating university cruise ship called *Seawise University*.

In 1972, while undergoing refurbishment in Hong Kong harbour, fire broke out aboard under unexplained circumstances and the ship was capsized by the water used to fight the fire. In 1973, the wreck was deemed an obstruction to shipping in the area, and so was partially scrapped where she lay.

QUEEN MARY 2 ON THE RIVER MERSEY WITH THE RMS BRITANNIA

An interesting comparison of scale between Cunard's first and latest transatlantic passenger ships.
The **Britannia** *could fit within the Britannia restaurant on the* **Queen Mary 2**. *Courtesy Cunard Line*

CUNARD'S THREE QUEENS IN SOUTHAMPTON FOR THE QUEEN'S DIAMOND JUBILEE

30x40 inches. Oil on canvas. Courtesy Cunard Line

CUNARD'S THREE QUEENS

Pictured on the River mersey liverpool celebrating 175th Anniversary. 25x35 inches Oil on canvas. Courtesy Cunard Line

QUEEN MARY VERANDAH GRILL 1936

20x16 inches. Oil on canvas. Courtesy of Frank Trumbour, private collection

QUEEN MARY BALLROOM

20x16 inches. Oil on canvas. Courtesy of Frank Trumbour, private collection

Case Study – Painting for the Captain

I was very privileged to hold command of the iconic ocean liner *Queen Mary 2* for six amazing years. As well as being a great honour, it was an interesting life as each day brought with it many challenges, opportunities and exciting experiences. It was therefore a great wrench when in 2017, I finally decided to swallow the anchor and retire. My wife Cheryl sailed with me throughout my time onboard *QM2* and so we both felt a great sadness stepping off her gangway for the last time, knowing our time onboard was at an end. The sadness was however, was soon to be replaced with a sense of liberation knowing I no longer held the responsibilities of command and my future days spent on the water would be carefree, as we enjoyed sailing our little Bavaria 34 *Scarlett* around the Solent.

To mark my retirement, Cheryl wanted to commission a painting of *QM2* from Robert. The subject of the painting would include my two favourite commands, *Queen Mary 2* and *Scarlett*. As a background we chose Calshot on Southampton Water, an area we often sail *Scarlett* on evenings when *QM2* sets off on another voyage. It's a great area to safely get very close to the ship and quite often the Captain onboard will sound the ships whistle in salute if he sees us out on the water.

Once our requirements were clearly defined, Robert soon produced a detailed sketch with *Scarlett* being set in the centre foreground, sailing by an outbound *Queen Mary 2* as she passes along the Calshot shoreline. The only additional detail was to include both our daughters, Karen and Danielle in the painting as they, along with their partners Rich and Ian, would normally make up our regular crew.

Within a few months Robert had completed his work and as he rarely saw his paintings set in their new home, he decided to deliver the painting personally.

Once removed from its protective wrapping and placed on the wall, we stood back in amazement at the breath-taking accuracy of the painting.

Robert had somehow managed to embrace all our requirements and then skilfully brush them onto canvas creating one perfect image that for us, encapsulates many vivid and wonderful memories.

For me, the image evokes memories of a late summers evening sail, the SW'ly wind is increasing, clouds are forming and there is a slight chill in the air. As we approach close to *QM2*, you sense the ships incredible power as she glides gracefully by, majestic, beautiful and massive, as she towers way above the top of our mast. On her bridge the Captain, Pilot and bridge team would be aware of us, but their attention is focused on increasing speed to twelve knots and preparing to make a significant turn to starboard, swinging the ship from Calshot Reach into the Thorn Channel, avoiding the dangerously shallow waters of Calshot Spit and the Bramble bank.

All too soon *QM2* passes clear, the last sounds of music and laughter linger in her wake, there is a final glimpse of waving passengers before they head to their staterooms to prepare for dinner and their first night at sea. Ahead of them lies the North Atlantic, the Captain and his crew would be scanning weather forecasts for the possibility of storms or dense fog and of course, preparing for the many cocktail parties and dinners. For me and my crew, it's time to give one final wave, furl the sails and turn *Scarlett* for home. My times on the Atlantic are now just memories and tonight there are no storms to be concerned about. All I have to do is take *Scarlett* safely to her berth and hope there is enough ice left in the freezer for us all to relax and enjoy a nice cool gin and tonic, mixed with *Scarlett's* own brand of White Star perfection.

Captain Kevin Oprey,
Master, Queen Mary 2

QUEEN MARY 2 PASSING YACHT SCARLETT

Pictured off Calshot, Southampton Water. 20x30 inches. Oil on canvas. Courtesy Captain Kevin Oprey

QUEEN MARY 2 – 'IN DEEP WATER.'
Mid-Atlantic. 20x30 inches. Oil on canvas. Courtesy Capt. Kevin Oprey

"*An amazing painting that really captures memories of a late evening on an east bound crossing of the North Atlantic Ocean. For me its about 1700hrs on our third day out of New York bound for Southampton, I have just finished working in my office and have decided to make my early evening visit the bridge to check that the 4-8 watch has settled in before I prepare for the evenings cocktail parties and dinner.*

After a brief chat with the Navigator, I walk out to my normal quiet spot on the starboard wing and spend some precious private time scanning the horizon. I check the forecasts and take time to gauge what weather the night would bring and whether I would need to adjust the ships course or speed, whilst subconsciously reflecting on the day's work.

Given the opportunity, I would gaze out of those bridge windows for hours on end, captivated by the ever-changing view as the ship forges her lonely way across the vast ocean. Passing through the changing weather patterns, the clouds constantly re-shape themselves as they fly overhead, on one side of the ship it looks darker as a squall develops, whilst on the other side a heavy rain-filled cloud is disappearing into the misty distance, revealing a patch of blue sky overhead and a welcome glimpse of a watery winter sun. All of this takes place before me in the space of just a few minutes, and as I leave the bridge, I know that tomorrow night I will get a completely different view of the North Atlantic, the dense fog of the Grand Banks of Newfoundland is astern of us, but ahead a storm or a lively gale could be brewing with strong winds and lashing rain that will whip the seas into a fury, but whatever the outlook, I know that Queen Mary 2 has the capability to deal with it."

QUEEN MARY 2 – 'IN DEEP WATER,'

Mid-Atlantic. 20x30 inches. Oil on canvas. Courtesy Capt. Kevin Oprey

CLASSIC SHIPS
WHEN SHIPS WERE BEAUTIFUL

MV. CALCHAS

In Belfast Lough. 25x35 inches. Oil on canvas. Private Collection

SS GORJISTAN
Pictured in the English Channel. 25x35 inches. Oil on canvas. Private collection

MV. MEMNON
Pictured at night passing the Sultan Shoal Lighthouse in the approaches to Singapore. 25x35 inches. Oil on canvas. Courtesy Mr B. Rubery

MV DURBAN CASTLE

Pictured at Galleons Reach, London. 30x40 inches. Oil on canvas. Private Collection

MV MANCHESTER SHIPPER

Pictured mid-Atlantic in heavy weather. 25x35 inches. Oil on canvas. Private collection.

NEW ZEALAND SHIPPING CO'S HINAKURA

Pictured off the Lloyd's Signal Station on the Lizard Peninsular. 20x16 inches. Oil on canvas board. Courtesy Anna Cox

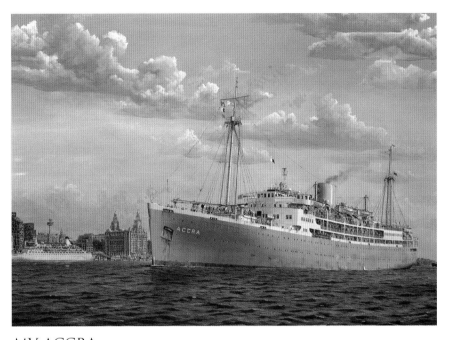

MV ACCRA

On the River Mersey. 25x35 inches. Oil on canvas. Private collection.

MV BENSTAC

Pictured unloading in the Far East, 30x40 inches. Oil on canvas. Courtesy Duncan Anderson.

MS SANTA ROSA

The Grace Line passenger ship Santa Barbara off the coast of Haiti in a heavy swell. 20x30 inches. Oil on canvas. courtesy Jack Fahy

53

MV APAPA

Discharging off the coast of Africa. 25x35 inches. Oil on canvas. Courtesy of David Kenwright

THE BOX SHIPS
A SHIPPING REVOLUTION

Before the advent of containerisation in the 1950s, break-bulk items were loaded, lashed, unlashed and unloaded from the ship one piece at a time. However, by grouping cargo into containers, 1,000 to 3,000 cubic feet (28 to 85 m3) of cargo, or up to about 64,000 pounds (29,000 kg), is moved at once and each container is secured to the ship once in a standardised way. Containerisation has increased the efficiency of moving traditional break-bulk cargoes significantly, reducing shipping time by 84% and costs by 35%. In 2001, more than 90% of world trade in non-bulk goods was transported in ISO containers. In 2009, almost one-quarter of the world's dry cargo was shipped by container, an estimated 125 million TEU or 1.19 billion metric tons worth of cargo.

The first ships designed to carrying standardised load units were used in the late 18th century in England. In 1766 James Brindley designed the box boat *Starvationer* with ten wooden containers, to transport coal from Worsley Delph to Manchester by Bridgewater Canal. Before the Second World War first container ships were used to carrying baggage's of the luxury passenger train from London to Paris, Golden Arrow / Flèche d'Or, in 1926 by Southern Railway. These containers were loaded in London or Paris and carried to ports, Dover or Calais, on flat cars in the UK and "CIWL Pullman Golden Arrow Fourgon of CIWL" in France.

The earliest container ships after the Second World War were converted oil tankers, built up from surplus T2 tankers after World War II. In 1951, the first purpose-built container vessels began operating in Denmark, and between Seattle and Alaska. The first commercially successful container ship was *Ideal X*, a T2 tanker, owned by Malcom McLean, which carried 58 metal containers between Newark, New Jersey and Houston, Texas, on its first voyage. In 1955, McLean built his company, McLean Trucking into one of United States' biggest freighter fleets. In 1955, he purchased the small Pan Atlantic Steamship Company from Waterman Steamship and adapted its ships to carry cargo in large uniform metal containers. On April 26, 1956, the first of these rebuilt container vessels, *Ideal X*, left the Port Newark in New Jersey and a new revolution in modern shipping resulted.

Container vessels eliminate the individual hatches, holds and dividers of the traditional general cargo vessels. The hull of a typical container ship is a huge warehouse divided into cells by vertical guide rails. These cells are designed to hold cargo in pre-packed units – containers. Shipping containers are usually made of steel, but other materials like aluminium, fibreglass or plywood are also used. They are designed to be entirely transferred to and from smaller coastal carriers, trains, trucks or semi-trailers (and so are carried by different modes of transport during one voyage, thus giving the name intermodal transport). There are several types of containers and they are categorised according to their size and functions.

Although containerisation caused a revolution in the world of shipping, its

MV ACT2

Pictured off the coast of New Zealand. 20x30 inches. Oil on canvas. Courtesy B. Rubery

introduction did not have an easy passage. Ports, railway (railroad in the US) companies, and shippers were concerned about the huge costs of developing the ports and railway infrastructure needed to handle container ships, and for the movement of containers on land by rail and road. Trade unions were concerned about massive job loss among port and dock workers at ports, as containers were sure to eliminate several manual jobs of cargo handling at ports. It took ten years of legal battles before container ships would be pressed into international service. In 1966, a container liner service from the US to the Dutch city of Rotterdam commenced. Containerisation changed not only the face of shipping, but it also revolutionised world trade as well. A container ship can be loaded and unloaded in a few hours compared to days in a traditional cargo vessel. This, besides cutting labour costs, has reduced shipping times between ports to a great extent; for example, it takes a few weeks instead of months for a consignment to be delivered from India to Europe and vice versa. It has also

ACT7 SEE OFF THE COAST OF NEW ZEALAND APPROACHING AUCKLAND

20x30 inches. Oil on canvas. Private collection

MV. NELE MAERSK ARRIVING IN NEW ZEALAND

20x16 inches. Oil on canvas. Private collection.

MV COSCO GLORY OFF VLISSINGEN

25x35 inches. Oil on canvas. Courtesy Rob Grool

resulted in less breakage due to less handling; also, there is less danger of cargo shifting during a voyage. As containers are sealed and only opened at the destination, pilferage and theft levels have been greatly reduced.

Containerisation has lowered shipping expense and decreased shipping time, and this has in turn helped the growth of international trade. Cargo that once arrived in cartons, crates, bales, barrels or bags now comes in factory sealed containers, with no indication to the human eye of their contents, except for a product code that machines can scan and computers trace. This system of tracking has been so exact that a two-week voyage can be timed for arrival with an accuracy of under fifteen minutes. It has resulted in such revolutions as on time guaranteed delivery and just in time manufacturing. Raw materials arrive from factories in sealed containers less than an hour before they are required in manufacture, resulting in reduced inventory expense.

Exporters load merchandise in boxes that are provided by the shipping companies. They are then delivered to the docks by road, rail or a combination of both for loading onto container ships. Prior to containerisation, huge gangs of men would spend hours fitting various items of cargo into different holds. Today, cranes, installed either on the pier or on the ship, are used to place containers on board the ship. When the hull has been fully loaded, additional containers are stacked on the deck.

Today's largest container ships such as the COSCO *Glory* measure 400 metres (1,300 ft) in length. They carry loads equal to the cargo-carrying capacity of sixteen to seventeen pre-World War II freighter ships. Today, about 90% of non-bulk cargo worldwide is transported by container, and modern container ships can carry over 21,000 TEU. As a class, container ships now rival crude oil tankers and bulk carriers as the largest commercial vessels on the ocean.

Case Study - Wan Hai Lines

Wan Hai Lines (Wàn Hǎi Hángyùn Gǔfèn Yǒuxiàn Gōngs) was founded in 1965 in Taiwan as a shipping company, its first vessel was the "LIBERTY" type bulk vessel christened *FOSMAR* and deployed between Japan and America for transporting steel. At the beginning, Wan Hai's business was mainly on the log transportation among Taiwan, Japan and the Southeast Asia. In 1966 they purchased their first log vessel a mini-bulker of 5,000 DWT from Japan christened which was named *WAN SHOU*.

In March 1969, WAN HAI's first new build log ship was delivered the M.V. *CHANG CHUN* deployed to Japan / Taiwan and Southeast Asia service.

In 1976, in order to respond to the rapid development of international trade in the Asia Pacific area and the trend of international transportation containerisation, Wan Hai has entered the business of container vessel shipping. More recently Wan Hai expanded its Asia shipping network to services to US, South America, Africa, and Middle East. In 1976 Wan Hai received its first full container vessel M.V. *MING CHUN* was deployed to Taiwan / Japan service which initiated WAN HAI's full container liner service. Wan Hai Lines has become the 12th largest player in the container shipping industry, with a fleet of seventy-two vessels and twenty-four chartered vessels and a capacity in excess of 180,000 TEUs.

In August 2018 an order was announced for twenty new ships, of which eight large 5-8000 TEU and twelve small feeder ships. Wan Hai have offices in over 20 countries the head office being in Kaohsiung, Taiwan.

MV GUADALUPE

A small container feeder vessel employed on the Gulf of Mexico between Florida and South America. 25x35 inches. Oil on canvas. Private Collection

WAN HAI 317 AT TAIPEI

35x45 inches. Oil on canvas. Courtesy Mr Charles Chen

WAN HAI 501

Passing the Tsing Ma Bridge outward bound from Hong Kong. 35x45 inches. Oil on canvas. Courtesy Mr Charles Chen

WAN HAI VESSELS IN KAOHSIUNG HARBOUR
30x60 inches. Oil on canvas. Courtesy Wan Hai Lines

THE GREAT OFFSHORE
THE OIL, GAS AND RENEWABLES INDUSTRY

As the World's demand for energy grew, so the need to locate oil and gas became ever more crucial. Offshore oil and gas production is far more challenging than land-based installations due to the remote and harsher environment.

Around 1891, the first submerged oil wells were drilled from platforms built on piles in the fresh waters of the Grand Lake St. Marys in Ohio. The wells were developed by small local companies such as Bryson, Riley Oil, German-American and Banker's Oil. Around 1896, the first submerged oil wells in salt water were drilled in the portion of the Summerland field extending under the Santa Barbara Channel in California. The wells were drilled from piers extending from land out into the channel.

In the early 1930s, the Texas Co., later Texaco (now Chevron) developed the first mobile steel barges for drilling in the brackish coastal areas of the Gulf of Mexico. In 1937, Pure Oil (now Chevron) and its partner Superior Oil (now ExxonMobil) used a fixed platform to develop a field 1 mile (1.6 km) offshore of Calcasieu Parish, Louisiana in 14 feet (4.3 m) of water.

In 1938, Humble Oil built a mile-long wooden trestle with railway tracks into the sea at McFadden Beach on the Gulf of Mexico, placing a derrick at its end - this was later destroyed by a hurricane.[5]

In 1945, concern for American control of its offshore oil reserves caused President Harry Truman to issue an Executive Order unilaterally extending American territory to the edge of its continental shelf, an act that effectively ended the 3-mile limit "freedom of the seas" regime.

In early 1947, Superior Oil erected a drilling and production platform in 20 feet (6.1 m) of water some 18 miles (29 km) off Vermilion Parish, La. But it was Kerr-McGee Oil Industries (now Anadarko Petroleum), as operator for partners Phillips Petroleum (ConocoPhillips) and Stanolind Oil & Gas (BP) that completed its historic Ship Shoal Block thirty-two well in October 1947, the first oil discovery drilled out of sight of land.

At this point it became clear that specialist supply vessels would be needed, not only to carry personal, equipment and stores out to these new 'rigs' but be able to do so in any weather. This was the birth of the offshore support vessel (OSV).

Over the years OSV's have become much more specialised and can be broken down into various ship types according to their design criteria.

A platform supply vessel (PSV) such as *Portosalvo* is a ship specially designed to supply offshore oil and gas platforms. These ships range from 50 to 100 meters in length and accomplish a variety of tasks. The primary function for most of these vessels is logistic support and transportation of goods, tools, equipment and personnel to and from offshore oil platforms and other offshore structures.

Fixed platforms were initially used for the offshore development (cont on page 66)

AGAINST THE ELEMENTS

An anchor handler in heavy weather. 40x30 inches. Oil on canvas. Courtesy David Kenwright

STRATHFARRAR AND THE CASTORO SEI
25x35 inches. Oil on canvas. Courtesy David Kenwright

THE FPSO PETROJARL KNARR

Pictured in operation in the North Sea. 30x40 inches. Oil on canvas. Courtesy Teekay Corporation

MV. SALVISCOUNT IN HEAVY WEATHER

20x30 inches. Oil on canvas. Courtesy Captain Ian Tew

A Viking Knarr, the original Viking cargo vessel which Petrojarl Knarr was named after. Painted for the naming ceremony of the Petrojarl Knarr

(from page 62) but the fields have gone deeper, floating production facilities have become the main solution for the offshore production. One of the most specialist type of vessel developed in recent years has been the Floating Production Storage and Offloading (FPSO) vessels. A FPSO vessel such as the Petrojarl Knarr is designed to receive hydrocarbons produced by itself or from nearby platforms or subsea template, process them, and store oil until it can be offloaded onto a tanker or, less frequently, transported through a pipeline. FPSOs are preferred in frontier offshore regions as they are easy to install, and do not require a local pipeline infrastructure to export oil.

A jack up rig or a self-elevating unit like the GMS *Endeavour* is a type of mobile platform that consists of a buoyant hull fitted with a number of movable legs, capable of raising its hull over the surface of the sea. The buoyant hull enables transportation of the unit and all attached machinery to a desired location. Once on location the hull is raised to the required elevation above the sea surface supported by the sea bed. The legs of such units may be designed to penetrate the sea bed, may be fitted with enlarged sections or footings, or may be attached to a bottom mat. Generally, jackup rigs are not self-propelled and rely on tugs or heavy lift ships for transportation.

Jack up platforms are used as exploratory drilling platforms and offshore and wind farm service platforms. Jack up platforms have been the most popular and numerous of various mobile types in existence.

The UT 704 was designed by Sigmund Borgundvåg as a multi-purpose anchor handling, tug, supply (AHTS) vessel with good sea keeping qualities and a large cargo capacity, particularly on deck. The first of ninety-one examples of the 65m long, 7,040bhp vessel to be built in Norway, and in yards around the world, was the Stad Scotsman for Stad Shipping of Alesund. This vessel is still operational, with many modifications and updates over the years, as the *Seabulk Condor* of Seacor Marine. The last UT 704 was delivered in 1993.

Following the initial success of the UT 704 further designs were developed in the mid-1970s such as the UT 705 (the first of thirty-one built being the Tender Carrier) and UT 706 platform supply vessels (PSVs). Meanwhile development of new propulsion arrangements was taking place – the UT 709 design of 1979 was the first to adopt diesel-electric propulsion, and in 1982 the UT 705 Stad Ulstein incorporated azimuth thrusters for the first time.

Before specialist towing and anchor handling ships were designed, deep water salvage tugs were employed to move barges and other floating construction equipment. *Salviscount* built in 1971 by Robb Caledon in Leith, Scotland. With a displacement of 3100 tons it was a very big tug indeed. Powered by two V-10 Crossley-Pielstick engines of 5,000 bhp each, it was driven by a massive 17-foot diameter Ka-Me-Wa controllable pitch prop in a Towmaster fixed nozzle.

The tug was owned by United Towing Ltd of Hull, and managed by their local tug company Humber Tugs Ltd. They ordered *Lloydsman* in response to the need to tow large ships, "supertankers" Tankers of 300,000 dwt were calling in British ports and there were no large British tugs to tow them if needed.

An expensive tug to operate, and facing stiff competition from the Dutch and Germans, United decided to build a replacement and sold *Lloydsman* to the Singapore based Selco Salvage in 1980. With Selco, and renamed *Salviscount*, it was used to tow large ships to scrap yards in Taiwan. On one particular tow of two VLCCs from Maracaibo to Kaohsiung, they were at sea for 173 days, at an average speed of 3.25 knots and covered 13,500 miles via the Cape of Good Hope. The *Salviscount* was sold for scrap and arrived at Gadani Beach on March 16, 1988.

Petrojarl Knarr is a Floating Production and Storage vessel (FPSO). She was built by Samsung in Korea for Teekay. The floating production vessel is 256 metres long and 48 metres wide. The ship has a production capacity of 63,000 barrels a day, and a storage capacity of 800,000 barrels. Accommodation is for 100 people.

She was named after a Viking Knarr which is the Old Norse term for a type of ship built for long sea voyages and used during the Viking expansion. The knarr was a cargo ship; the hull was wider, deeper and shorter than a longship, and could take more cargo and be operated by smaller crews. They were built with a length of about 16 m (54 ft), a beam of 5 m (15 ft), and a hull capable of carrying up to 24 tons. It was primarily used to transport trading goods like walrus ivory, wool, timber, wheat, furs and pelts, armour, slaves, honey, and weapons. It was also used to supply food, drink, weapons and armour to warriors and traders along their journeys across the Baltic, the Mediterranean and other seas. Knerrir routinely crossed the North Atlantic carrying livestock such as sheep and horses, and stores to Norse settlements in Iceland, Greenland and Finland as well as trading goods to trading posts in the British Isles, Continental Europe and possibly as far as the Middle East

The deepwater construction vessel *Aegir* is owned by Heerema Marine Contractors and was christened on September 2013. She is equipped for a wide range of operations including J-lay and reel pipelaying, with a payload of 4,500 metric tons. Her main crane has a lift capacity of 4,000 metric tonnes and lowering equipment can reach a depth of 3,500 meters. The monohull is designed for fast transit speed and optimum motion characteristics in operation. The vessel can accommodate 289 persons.

The Russian Ministry of Gas ordered the self- propelled crane vessel *Stanislav Yudin* from the Finnish Wartsilla shipyard in 1982. The crane fitted on the stern of the vessel was designed by GustoMSC and built by Kone Oy in Finland.

The vessel built by Wartsilla has a length of approx. 183 m, a width of 36 m and a depth of 13 m. The crane was originally designed with two 800-ton *(cont on page 72)*

PETROJARL KNARR LEAVING THE SHIPYARD

30x40 inches. Oil on canvas. Courtesy Teekay Corporation

GMS ENDEAVOUR AT NIGHT
30x40 inches. Oil on canvas. courtesy GMS, UAE.

HEEREMA AEGIR
Pictured in the North Sea. 30x40 inches. Oil on canvas. Courtesy Offshore Shipbrokers.

GMS ENDEAVOUR HELI DECK VIEW
30x40 inches. Oil on canvas. Courtesy GMS, UAE.

SEAWAY HEAVY LIFT, THE SEAWAY UDIN AND SEAWAY STASHNOV

Pictured during a heavy lift operation. 30x40 inches. Oil on canvas. Courtesy Offshore Shipbrokers.

MAERSK CONNECTOR
Pictured aground during the installation of the Walney windfarm. 20x30 inches. Oil on canvas. Courtesy Damen Shipyard Group

SAFE BOREAS UNDER TOW

25x35 inches. Oil on canvas. Courtesy Offshore Shipbrokers

*CS **Electra** pictured off Rio*

*Sketch of the **Highland Endurance***

(from page 66) main hooks, which could be operated separately, a 400-ton auxiliary hook and a trolley with a 30 ton hook which could travel along the length of the box girder crane boom. To lift the maximum load of 1,600 tons, the two main hooks can be used independently allowing an angle with the vertical of up to 15° or they can be coupled together by a hoisting beam with a 1,600-ton hook.

Built in 2010, GMS Endeavour and her sister vessels *Enterprise* and *Endurance* is a self-propelled, self-elevating accommodation DP II jack up barge. It is capable of providing well service, construction, installation and accommodation capabilities for up to 142 persons. GMS *Endeavour* has a 230 ton crane and can operate in water depths of up to 65m. She is one of four exact sister vessels built by GMS.

Built in 1945 by Swan, Hunter and Wigham Richardson Ltd. The CS *Electra* was the last of the four cable ships built for the Admiralty during World War II. Fitted with three tanks with a total coiling capacity of 11,775 cubic feet. A cargo hold was fitted forward of the No 1 tank for stowing cable buoys, grapnels etc. Three bow sheaves 3 ft 6 in. in diameter.

In 1946 sold to Cable & Wireless and renamed *Electra* (2). Based in the West Indies until sold to the Commercial Cable Company in 1959 and renamed *Cable Guardian*. Sold for scrap in 1964, arriving at Inverkeithing on 21 June 1964 for breaking up.

MV **Maersk Connector** is Maersk's first cable-lay vessel specifically designed to be intentionally grounded as part of a cable-lay operation. She represents a new generation of cable-laying vessel, developed as a flexible platform for both transport and installation work offshore. The 138m long and 27m wide vessel has the capability of grounding out on the seabed with its seven points mooring system. This eliminates the need to also charter a separate shallow water cable-lay vessel and minimises the number of cable joints required. *Maersk Connector* has state-of-the-art equipment, including a 7,000-tonne capacity cable carousel and a 100 tonne subsea crane and can also accommodate ninety people.

The *Safe Boreas* is the most advanced and efficient harsh environment accommodation vessel in the world, constructed to comply with Norwegian regulations.

Safe Boreas was built at Jurong Shipyard Pte Ltd. in Singapore and is constructed according to the GVA 3000E design and is equipped with a DP3 (dynamic

positioning) system as well as 12-point mooring arrangement. This allows for operations in harsh environments both in DP and anchored mode, providing maximum cost efficiency and flexibility.

The vessel has the capacity to accommodate 450 persons in single man cabins. The layout of the unit is unique, with two large internal atriums allowing natural daylight into cabins, mess room and recreational areas.

Kroonborg was built in 2015 by Royal Niestern Sander shipyard in the Netherlands and is long-term chartered to work in the Southern North Sea for Dutch oil and gas company Nederlandse Aardolie Maatschappij BV (NAM) over the next decade. This "Walk-to-Work" vessel, as the name suggests, features a motion compensated crane that allows offshore workers to be easily transferred aboard an unmanned offshore platforms, but she is much more than that.

Measuring nearly 80 meters, Wagenborg describes *Kroonborg* as "a workshop, storage, hotel and way of transport. She offers accommodation facilities to sixty people, including two crews of twenty technicians."

In July of 1958, Houston entrepreneur Hy Bird, armed with business acumen and a modest amount of capital, incorporated Gulf Interstate Company. It began business operations in January of the following year with a net worth of $431,000. At the outset, Gulf Interstate was essentially a pipeline engineering firm. One of its initial projects was the engineering and construction of the Transwestern Pipeline that originated in West Texas and terminated in California. The $200 million project was completed in 1960. Also, in 1960, the firm began investing in office buildings in downtown Houston. Later real estate investments included industrial and mixed-use properties in Buffalo, New York, as well as interests in resort properties in Arizona, Colorado, Hawaii, Acapulco and Cozumel. Ever vigilant for other strategic opportunities, Gulf Interstate ventured into the wholesale air conditioning and heating business and later into the pollution control industry. When the returns were not deemed satisfactory, the company exited those businesses to free up funds for other investments.

In 1969, Gulf Interstate became active in an international venture – a marine terminal in England. The terminal, or tank farm, was located at the mouth of the Tyne

SUPPLY VESSEL PORTOSALVO

The Italian owned GulfMark operated platform supply vessel is pictured departing Aberdeen into the 'teeth of a gale'. 30x40 inches. Oil on canvas. Courtesy GulfMark

HIGHLAND ROVER

*Pictured with the cable-lay vessel **Solitaire** in the North Sea. 25x35 inches. Oil on canvas*

River near Newcastle. It consisted of twenty-six storage tanks capable of accommodating more than seventy ships annually.

In 1971, Gulf Interstate got a glimpse of its future when it acquired a 45 percent interest in Gulf Overseas Marine Corporation, a Louisiana-based firm that furnished utility boats to service offshore drilling rigs in the Gulf of Mexico. Company president Farrile Young noted, "With approximately 100 rigs operating in the Gulf today and each requiring two or more service and supply boats, this boating operation should play a major role in Gulf Interstate's continuous programme of expansion. Due to the growth in the number of rigs operating in the Gulf, Gulf Overseas Marine is currently negotiating for an additional supply boat."

In 1990, the company purchased the marine division of Offshore Logistics, Inc. This acquisition formed the nucleus of what became the Gulf Offshore Marine Division, which operated eleven offshore service vessels in three geographic areas: The North Sea, Southeast Asia and Brazil. The purchase of this business represented an initial move, as a direct operating entity, into the international oilfield service industry. The acquisition gave the company a significant presence in the most active offshore exploration and development markets in the world, while avoiding any exposure to the less favourable conditions in the Gulf of Mexico.

Painting of GulfMark's 'G' logo incorporating various vessels of the fleet.
30x40 inches. Oil on canvas. Courtesy GulfMark

as extensive under-deck tank facilities for transporting liquid products including fuel, drinking water and specialty fluids used in drilling and production. The largest supply vessels have specially designed and configured deck areas for carrying large diameter pipe to remote sites in support of major subsea pipeline construction programmes. Additionally, these vessels are capable of performing survey, ROV (remote operated vehicle) and other specialised support services.

Gulf's fleet consisted principally of supply vessels. The objective was to provide the highest level of service with modern, safe, technologically advanced equipment, especially to the more stable production and development activities of the major international oil companies. A new generation built to order Gulf's newly constructed vessels represented a new generation of supply vessels. The *Highland Piper*, delivered in 1996, was a completely new design, the UT 755, developed to be cost-effective in meeting current and projected routine offshore requirements. Features of this design were a disproportionately large deck area and enhanced under-deck capacities, which were made possible by concentrating the forward superstructure within the bow area, leaving the entire parallel cargo rail and midbody sections available exclusively for cargo operation. Tank capacities were further increased as a result of concentrated efforts to find and eliminate every possible below-deck area of unused or dead space. In addition, the working deck environment was improved by the deeper hull form and provision of a fully plated cargo rail instead of a pipe structure. This both provides a weather break and is preferred by crane operators, who dislike the pipe structure.

The UT 755 could operate much more efficiently than previous designs, requiring only two-thirds the cargo to operate cost-effectively. These vessels enabled the company to continue the objective of building on its strengths in servicing niche markets in the North Sea, Southeast Asia and South America.

On the leadership front, Bruce Streeter, who had been with the company since 1990, was named President. A Growing Fleet GulfMark's fleet has continued to grow. A construction programme that was completed in 1999 provided expansion of activity into Brazil, an entry into West Africa and the first contract for a modern platform supply vessel (PSV) in Asia. A programme initiated in 2000 added nine new vessels. A programme launched in 2006 added two vessels to the North Sea operations in 2007 and ten vessels to Southeast Asia by 2008. With the acquisition of Rigdon Marine in 2008, GulfMark owned and managed more than ninety technologically sophisticated, high specification vessels. In 2011, GulfMark launched a programme to add seven of the world's most advanced PSVs to the fleet. The last of the newly ordered vessels was scheduled for delivery in 2015. Mr. Butters noted, "Rather than merely buying more vessels, we're investing in craft that set the standards for technology and efficiency, widening margins for ourselves and our clients."

Weathering the Financial Storm In 2008, as the energy market continued to be affected by the upheaval in the financial markets, GulfMark *(cont on page 79)*

Recognising that its business had fundamentally changed, the company changed its name as well—to GulfMark International, Inc. The name was chosen to recognise the leadership and contributions of the company's long-serving and revered Chairman, the late Mark Millard. GulfMark's new marine services division, Gulf Offshore Marine supported a broad range of offshore exploration, drilling and production activities. Its services included towing and positioning of mobile drilling rigs; anchor handling; transporting personnel and supplies to offshore platforms; and supporting offshore pipe laying and construction projects.

Success Amidst the Storm During 1991, the US petroleum industry was under siege. Oil markets were volatile and unstable. Natural gas prices reached lows that had not been seen for over a decade. Major oil companies reduced domestic exploration expenditures. The exodus by the smaller independent operators continued, and new regulatory and environmental restrictions were enacted. All these factors converged in 1991, and the domestic drilling rig count plunged to its lowest historically recorded level.

Despite this, the fleet grew from the original eleven vessels in 1990 to twenty-five by year-end 1993. Much of the dramatic increase resulted from the acquisition of BP Shipping Ltd., the wholly owned marine services arm of British Petroleum (BP). The Vessels of Gulf Offshore Marine Then as now, Gulf's vessels were generally of two types: platform supply and anchor handling. They each perform a variety of functions. Anchor handlers are characterised by higher horsepower and special equipment such as large towing winches. This type of vessel is used particularly during the field exploration phase to move and reposition large mobile drilling rigs. Platform supply vessels have large deck areas which are used for carrying cargoes or containers, as well

HIGHLAND DEFENDER

In rough seas off the North East of Scotland. 25x35 inches. Oil on canvas

HIGHLAND EAGLE

Pictured undertaking windfarm maintenance. 20x30 inches. Oil on canvas

GULFMARK OFFSHORE VESSEL

In operation in the North Sea. 20x16 inches. Watercolour

HIGHLAND FORTRESS

Pictured at anchor for her christening in the Norwegian Fjords, 2001. 25x35 inches. Oil on canvas

AUSTRAL ABROLHOS

Pictured at Rio De Janerio. 20x30 inches. Oil on canvas

HIGHLAND PRINCESS, CHIEFTAIN AND PRESTIGE

Pictured at Aberdeen. 30x40 inches. Oil on canvas

'OPERATION STRETCH'

*the GulfMark vessel **Knockout** shown cut in half with a new centre section added, Louisiana 2012. 20x30 inches. Oil on canvas.*

GULFMARK OFFSHORE VESSEL IN OPERATION

Gulf of Mexico. 20x16 inches. Watercolour.

(from page 75) continued to focus on strengthening its balance sheet and securing the future contract position of the fleet.

GulfMark's current fleet consists of the larger type of open ocean craft that oil and gas producers will need as they venture farther offshore, into deeper water, and into ever harsher environments. From platform supply vessels (PSVs), anchor handling tugs (AHTs) and fast supply vessels (FSVs) to multi-purpose specialty vessels (MPSVs), the fleet of 70 owned GulfMark-flagged vessels remains among the youngest and most technologically advanced fleets in the industry, thus ensuring that GulfMark can continue to provide maximum performance in all climates around the world. As producers explore tough new production environments such as the Falkland Islands, the east coast of Africa, the Indian Ocean and the Barents Sea, GulfMark's larger, ruggedly built vessels are the types customers need to support various types of offshore projects.

In late 2018, GulfMark Offshore merged with Tidewater to create the world's largest offshore support fleet.

MV KROONBORG

Pictured during rig maintenance in the North Sea. 20x30 inches. Oil and canvas. Courtesy of Wagenborg BV.

HIGHLAND ENDURANCE

Pictured towing a semi-submersible rig in the Caribbean, June 2017. 25x35 inches. Oil on canvas

THE GULFMARK VESSEL HERCULES
Pictured in the Mississippi River for her naming in 2016. 25x35 inches. Oil on canvas

MIAMI SHIPS

The port of Miami boasts the title "cruise capital of the world" and is the busiest cruise/passenger port in the world. It accommodates the operations of such major cruise lines as Carnival, Royal Caribbean and Norwegian Cruise Line.

In the early 1900s, Government Cut was dredged along with a new channel to what now is known as Bicentennial Park in downtown Miami. This new access to the mainland created the Main Channel which greatly improved the shipping access to the new port. From these original dredging spoils which were disposed on the south side of the new Main Channel, new islands were inadvertently created which later became Dodge, Lummus and Sam's Island along with several other smaller islands.

As the port grew through the years as a result of the improved shipping access and growth of the South Florida community, it also needed additional lands to expand its operation. As such, on April 5, 1960 the Dade County Board of Commissioners approved Resolution No. 4830, "Joint Resolution Providing for Construction of Modern Seaport Facilities at Dodge Island Site" which on April 6, 1960 the City of Miami approved the same as City Resolution No. 31837 to construct the new Port of Miami. Soon thereafter, work began on constructing the new port on Dodge Island by expanding the island and joining it to other islands in the general vicinity. Then upon construction of the new seawalls, transit shed 'A', the administration building and a new vehicle and railroad bridge, the operations were transferred from the mainland port to the new port on Dodge Island. Thereafter through the years, additional fill material from dredging enlarged the islands of Lummus and Sam's along with the filling of the North, South and NOAO slips, creating the new port which is built on a completely man-made island. As the "Cargo Gateway of the Americas", the port primarily handles containerized cargo with small amounts of break-bulk, vehicles and industrial equipment. It is the largest container port in the state of Florida and ninth in the United States. As a world-class port, PortMiami is among an elite group of ports in the world which cater to both cruise ships and containerised cargo.

PortMiami is an important contributor to the local south Florida and state economies. Over four million cruise passengers pass through the Port, 7.4 million tons of cargo and over 1 million twenty-foot equivalent units (TEU) (FY 2004/2005) of intermodal container traffic move through the seaport per year. This combination of cruise and cargo activities supports approximately 176,000 jobs and has an economic impact in Miami-Dade County of over $17 billion, $14 billion of which is generated by its cargo operations.

S.S. Bahama Star

In 1959, Eastern acquired *Arosa Star* (Arosa Line) through the McCormick Shipping Corporation for approximately $510,000.

She was renamed *Bahama Star* and after a refit was placed on the Miami-Nassau run. Two years later, the company purchased the tiny Ariadne from Hamburg America.

She was placed on luxury cruises to the Caribbean, and to enhance the ship's appeal she was completely redecorated, refurnished and air-conditioned in 1963. Ownership of Eastern changed hands again in 1962 when W.R. Lovett of Jacksonville, Florida, purchased the company, which accounted for the white 'L' on the blue diamond which

BAHAMA STAR

Approaching her berth at Miami in the early 1960s. 20x16 inches. Oil on canvas. Courtesy Jeff Macklin, private collection

appeared on the funnels during Lovett's ownership.

The *Bahama Star* was put on three-day, four-day and seven-day cruises, and *Bahama Star* remained on the Nassau service. A seven-day cruise aboard the *Ariadne* during the summer of 1965 ranged from $160 (£57) for inside accommodation without facilities to $425 (£152) for the owner's suite. A four- day cruise in *Bahama Star* ranged from $95 to $160, and a three-day cruise from $80 to $130.

For the next seven years the itinerary of the ships did not alter. With the acquisition of Zim line's S.S. *Jerusalem*, renamed *New Bahama* Star, in 1969, S.S. Bahama Star was sold to Pacific interests and finally lost in a hurricane.

The end of American ownership of Eastern Steamship came in 1970 when the Norwegian shipping firm of Gotass-Larsen purchased the line. In 1981 the company was restyled Eastern Cruises, and later in 1983 amalgamated with Western Cruise Lines

TUGBOAT MARY BELCHER

The Miami based tugboat during towing operations in the Port of Miami in the mid-nineteen eighties. 20x16 inches Oil on canvas. Courtesy Jeff Macklin, private collection

NEW BAHAMA STAR

Inward bound to Miami, passing Great Isaac Light, Bahamas at midnight. 25x35 inches. Oil on canvas. Courtesy Jeff Macklin

and Sundance Cruises to form Admiral Cruises.

The *Queen of Nassau* was built as the Yarmouth in 1927 by William Cramp & Sons Ship and Engine Building Company in Philadelphia, Pennsylvania. The Yarmouth and her sister, Evangeline were designed for the US to New Brunswick and Nova Scotia coastal trade. Both ships served as troop transports in World War II and after the war were flagged out and eventually ended up in Miami sailing to the Bahamas and the Caribbean.

By the mid 1960's the *Queen of Nassau*, now the *Yarmouth* and her sister the *Yarmouth Castle*, formerly the *Evangeline* made up a fleet of antiquated cruise ships sailing to the Bahamas from Miami. The tragic fire and sinking of the *Yarmouth Castle* 13 miles from Great Stirrup Cay the night of November 13, 1965 with the loss of ninety lives was the beginning of the end for the old and obsolete ships sailing from Miami.

New safety regulations adopted after the sinking of the *Yarmouth Castle* were the catalyst for the cruise industry that thrives today. New, modern, purpose-built cruise ships would soon replace the old and tired fleet mates of the *Queen of Nassau*. The *Queen of Nassau* and her fleet mates that were once owned by F. Leslie Fraser proved the economic viability of year-round cruising from the Port of Miami.

The *Bahama Star* was built as the *Borinquen*, designed by Theodore E. Ferris and was built at the Bethlehem Shipbuilding Corporation's Fore River Shipyard in Quincy, Massachusetts 20 January 1930, launched 24 September 1930 and completed in 1931 with delivery 20 February 1931. The ship's name came from the Taino language name, *Borikén*, for the island of Puerto Rico. She was delivered to the Atlantic, Gulf & West Indies Steamship Lines for operation by AGWI's subsidiary, New York & Porto Rico Line.

The ship was propelled by single, impulse-reaction type, reduction geared turbines furnished with steam by oil fired tube boilers for about 6,500 horsepower. She arrived in New York 22 February 1931 and began her working career with a maiden voyage from New York to San Juan, Puerto Rico and Santo Domingo, Dominican Republic

which would become her regular scheduled route.[5][9]

During World War II she was requisitioned from Agwilines, Inc. by the War Shipping Administration on 31 December 1941 with Agwilines as the operator. On 6 May 1944 Borinquen was transferred to direct War Department operation by the Transportation Corps under bareboat charter as the USAT *Borinquen* until returned to Agwilines 14 June 1946. She had a capacity for 1,289 troops and 404 medical patients. USAT *Borinquen* was one of the Army transports at Normandy.

After the war she was sold to the Bull Steamship Company and renamed the *Puerto Rico*.

In 1954 she was purchased by the Arosa Line (*Compañía Internacional Transportadora* – owned by Nicolo Rizzi, a Swiss-Italian financier) and operated as the extensively rebuilt *Arosa Star* until 1958. During this period, she transported immigrants from northern Europe to Canada and the United States, with regular ports of call at Halifax, Quebec City, Montreal and New York City. With the advent of affordable air travel, the market for hauling immigrants quickly disappeared and the *Arosa Line* went bankrupt.

In the years 1959–69, she was operated for Eastern Steamship Lines as the *Bahama Star*, sailing primarily between Florida and the Bahamas. During this period, the *Bahama Star* managed to rescue 489 people from the burning SS *Yarmouth Castle*, another cruise ship; ninety people perished in the blaze. In a bizarre twist of fate, this accident led to changes to the maritime regulations pertaining to such ships at the Geneva Convention of 1964, outlawing the operation of passenger vessels with wooden super-structures. The cost of complying with the new regulations proved too expensive, so the ship was sold to the Western Steamship Company.

She was renamed again, this time to *La Jenelle*. The new owners brought her to Port Hueneme, California, where they intended to sell her. Some say that plans were underway to make her a floating restaurant/casino. Others claim she was to be sold to an Indonesian shipping firm, but neither plan materialised. By 1970, she was anchored outside the harbour to avoid expensive docking fees while efforts were made to find a buyer. On April 13, her luck ran out. That particular day was blustery, with a northwest

SS NORWAY BERTHED AT MIAMI

25x35 inches. Oil on canvas. Courtesy of Jeff Macklin, private collection

gale ripping the tops off the waves. Seas broke everywhere, and nearly everyone was in port. *La Jenelle's* starboard anchor – the only one out – began to drag. There were only two crewmen aboard, and they were unable to stop her drift. Only 23 minutes later, she struck the sandy beach west of the Port Hueneme breakwater, her stern just missing the rocks. *La Jenelle* began to list as she took on water. The crew stayed aboard, attempting to pump her dry so she could be righted, but the seas were pouring in from many smashed portholes and windows making their efforts fruitless. A helicopter arrived to rescue them as the ship settled further into the sand.

The *La Jenelle* proved to be quite an attraction. Crowds flocked to Silver Strand Beach to see the stranded behemoth. Surfers paddled out to the stricken ship to wander among passageways canted at impossible angles, reminiscent of the film, Poseidon Adventure. Salvers picked over her bones, tearing away loose brass hardware and anything else of value. Her plates began to buckle under the incessant pounding of the surf as one compartment after another was destroyed.[17] A fire, perhaps started by vandals, gutted her interior. *La Jenelle* became a real hazard in time, for it was impossible to keep people off her. Eventually a souvenir hunter fell from the wreck and was drowned. By then, the owners had faded from the scene during the litigation that follows such an incident. A United States Navy team cut the top off the ship and brought in rocks to fill in the carcass. *La Jenelle* was transformed into a new arm for the Port of Hueneme breakwater.

SS New Bahama Star, 'A Night to Remember'

By Jeff Macklin, Florida

The SS New Bahama Star was built as the SS *Jerusalem* for the Zim Israel and Navigation Company entering service in 1958. The SS *Jerusalem* was designed for Mediterranean service. She was built by the German shipyard Deutsche Werft in Hamburg, Germany as part of the war reparations for the Israelis that included three other passenger/cargo ships of similar sized and design. As built, the *Jerusalem* had a gross tonnage of 9,920 tons, a length overall of 488 feet a beam of 65 feet and a draft of 21 feet. She was steamed powered, DR geared turbines to twin screws gave the ship a service speed of 18.5 knots. Her passenger capacity was 573 passengers, 102 in first class, 471 in tourist class.

In 1964 the *Jerusalem* was refitted for more extensive cruising. In 1966 she was chartered to the Peninsular & Occidental Company of Miami, on a 3-year charter for the Miami to Nassau run, sailing as the SS *Miami*. In 1968 the charter was cancelled, and Zim Lines placed the Jerusalem on the market. The ship was purchased by Eastern Steamship Lines of Miami to replace the SS *Bahama Star*. The ship received a major refit at Jacksonville Shipyard costing 5 million dollars.

The SS *New Bahama Star* sailed on her maiden voyage from Miami on March 10, 1969. She could now carry 755 passengers in one class. Economic growth in the early 1970's was weak, unemployment was high, and the oil crisis of 1973 caused high inflation, so it was tough times for the cruise industry. On October 27, 1974 the *New Bahama Star* suffered boiler damage which afected the ship's reliability. Due to all of the above, and the fact Eastern Steamship Lines also had the *Emerald Seas* which was a larger and well-appointed ship on the same 3 and 4 day itinerary, Eastern Steamship Lines abruptly withdrew the SS *Bahama Star*, as she had been renamed from service on January 6, 1975. A combination of rising fuel and food costs, mechanical issues and poor bookings were given as reasons for the ship being taken out of service.

In 1975 the *Bahama Star* was sold to Venozolana De Crucerous for Caribbean cruises under the Venezuela Flag and she was renamed the *Bonaire Star*. The ship promptly went into lay up in Mobile, Alabama and never sailed again. She was sold numerous times for scrap and was being towed to Kaohsiung, Taiwan by the tug Jantar when she sank in route in the Pacific Ocean on October 3, 1979.

Robert Lloyd's painting represents the *New Bahama Star* sailing on a course of WNW in the Northwest Providence Channel towards Miami after leaving Nassau a few hours earlier. The date is Sunday night, March 26, 1972. Great Issac Light to her port quarter.

I was on board that night, sailing with my best high school friend John on this 3-day cruise from Miami to Nassau. The cruise was a high school graduation gift from our parents. Our inside cabin, #331, all the way at the stern on the lowest passenger deck was cheap, small and cold. Both John and I were excited about the cruise.

A couple of good friends drove us down to the ship and they were allowed on board to see us . My cruise began by having a Singapore Sling with Peggy in the "Bahama Lounge", as we were too young to legally drink in Florida at the time, we took advantage of being on a foreign flag ship.

My cruise ended as I stood on top of the bridge in solitary observation of the sea and sky as we steamed back to Miami on Sunday night. It was a perfect night at sea, a slight swell from a following sea gently pushed the ship on her course, the moon was almost full and the breeze was cool. A young Bahamian security guard making his rounds interrupted my solitude by telling me I was not allowed on top of the bridge after dark. Soon however, we were engaged in a serious yet congenial conversation about God, the fate of mankind and the meaning of life. A very extra ordinary conversation for two strangers to have. After a while my new friend left to complete his rounds. I remained on top of the bridge to reflect on our conversation and to enjoy the complete peace and tranquillity of the night. The night to me was ethereal, a celestial and spiritual experience.

In my conversations with Robert Lloyd I compliment him on his ability to 'capture a moment in time' with his paintings. The ships Robert has painted for me all have been part of my life and therefore, his paintings create for me emotional and tangible feelings as his paintings represent the ship and the moment in time so well. With this painting Robert has been able to 'capture an entire night at sea' that was very special.

STARWARD

Pictured at dawn as she approaches Miami. 25x35 inches. Oil on canvas. Courtesy Jeff Macklin, private collection

Memories of the MS. Starward
By Captain Kaare Bakke

I joined the *Starward* end of June 1975. Back then we had a car deck and carried a maximum of 30 - 40ft containers on chassis and 3- 20 ft if we stored well. Loading and discharging via roll on roll-off via stern gate and stern ramp. We had to hook up for reefer and freezer trailers as well. Loaded in Miami for Port au Prince, Montego Bay and Nassau. Some cargo or mostly empty trailers to return to Miami.

The car deck was equipped with one extra car deck to be lowered down with hydraulic power loading total space of 208 American Size cars over two decks.

Vessel was equipped with two cranes on the forecastle with 10 ton cranes through the cargo hatch opening down to the car deck. However, the use of cranes were not used for cargo operation. The vessel picked up the port of Miami pilot around 6-00AM and alongside about 7-00AM. During fall of 1976, the vessel was about 4 weeks in drydock in Jacksonville the aft part of the sun deck and boat deck were extended including various other refurbishments.

The car deck was eliminated in 1978, I believe, thereby 106 cabins for guests were installed on Biscayne and Caribbean Decks. Also a nice theatre with seating for 204 were constructed in the middle of the vessel on these two decks as well. 5 life rafts with launching cranes were installed on each side in order to increase the lifesaving appliances to accommodate more passengers and crew. Also, one more diesel generator was installed for the extra power supply needed.

I was Staff Capt. on board *Starward* in September of 1979, when the *Skyward* had a fire in the auxiliary engine room just prior to arrival Miami. The *Starward* disembarked their passengers in Miami as fast as possible then went back out and evacuated the *Skyward's* passengers and their luggage via *Starward's* lifeboats while manoeuvring around in the Gulf current. The *Starward* was scheduled for drydock in Jacksonville that day, so the *Skyward* took that spot and *Starward* returned to Miami and disembarked the *Skyward's* passengers and embarked her passengers for the next cruise. That was probably the hardest day of work I have been subjected to.

I believe the next major refurbishment of the vessel took place in 1984. I left the on board service as Captain in November of 1983 and started working in the office until April 8.2005. In my opinion the *Starward* was the best maintained ship in the NCL fleet of the four white ships at that time.

SS. NORWAY

Pictured in dry dock, Blohm+Voss Shipyard, Hamburg, Germany. September 1984, 25x35 inches. Oil on canvas. Courtesy Jeff Macklin, private collection

SS. QUEEN OF NASSAU

Pictured in the Bahamas, 20x30 inches oil on canvas courtesy of Jeff Macklin.

EVERYTHING BULK

The bulk carrier or colloquially, bulker, is a merchant ship specially designed to transport unpackaged bulk cargo, such as grains, coal, ore, and cement, in its cargo holds. Since the first specialised bulk carrier was built in 1852, economic forces have led to continued development of these ships, resulting in increased size and sophistication. Today's bulk carriers are specially designed to maximise capacity, safety, efficiency, and durability.

Today, bulk carriers make up 15–17% of the world's merchant fleet and range in size from single hold mini-bulk carriers to mammoth ore ships able to carry 400,000 metric tons of deadweight known as ValeMax.

Over half of all bulk carriers have Greek, Japanese, or Chinese owners and more than a quarter are registered in Panama. South Korea is the largest single builder of bulk carriers, and 82% of these ships were built in Asia.

Bulk cargo can be very dense, corrosive, or abrasive. This can present safety problems: cargo shifting, spontaneous combustion, and cargo saturation can threaten a ship. The use of ships that are old and have corrosion problems has been linked to a spate of bulk carrier sinkings in the 1990s, as have the bulk carrier's large hatchways. While important for efficient cargo handling, these allow the entry of large volumes of water in storms if their hatch covers become loose or if a ship is endangered by sinking. New international regulations have since been introduced to improve ship design and inspection, and to streamline the process of a crew's abandoning ship.

Before specialised bulk carriers were developed, shippers had two methods to move bulk goods by ship. In the first method, longshoremen loaded the cargo into sacks, stacked the sacks onto pallets, and put the pallets into the cargo hold with a crane. The second method required the shipper to charter an entire ship and spend time and money to build plywood bins into the holds. Then, to guide the cargo through the small hatches, wooden feeders and shifting boards had to be constructed. These methods were slow and labour-intensive. As with the container ship, the problem of efficient loading and unloading has driven the evolution of the bulk carrier.

Bulk carriers are segregated into six major size categories: small, handysize, handymax, panamax, capesize, and very large. Very large bulk and ore carriers fall into the capesize category but are often considered separately.

Categories also occur in regional trades, such as Kamsarmax: Maximum length overall 229 meters refers to a new type of ships, larger than panamax, that are suitable for berthing at the Port of Kamsar (Republic of Guinea), where the major loading terminal of bauxite is restricted to vessels not more than 229 meters.

Newcastlemax: Maximum beam 50 meters, and maximum length overall of 300 meters Refers to the largest vessel able to enter the port of Newcastle, Australia at about 185,000 DWT

Malaccamax: LOA 330 m / 20 m draft / 300,000 DWT, Refers to the largest vessel that can pass through the Straits of Malacca.

Dunkirkmax: Maximum allowable beam = 45 m / LOA 289 m. max (175,000 DWT approx.) for the eastern harbour lock in the Port of Dunkirk (France)

Mini-bulk carriers are prevalent in the category of small vessels with a capacity of under 10,000 DWT. Mini-bulk carriers carry from 500 to 2,500 tons, have a single hold, and are designed for river transport. They are often built to be able to pass under bridges and have small crews of three to eight people.

Handysize and Handymax ships are general purpose in nature. These two segments represent 71% of all bulk carriers over 10,000 DWT. Handymax ships are typically 150–200 m in length and 52,000 – 58,000 DWT with five cargo holds and four cranes.

The size of a Panamax vessel is limited by the Panama canal's lock chambers, which can accommodate ships with a beam of up to 32.31 m, a length overall of up to 294.13 m, and a draft of up to 12.04 m.

Capesize ships are too large to traverse the Panama Canal and must round Cape Horn to travel between the Pacific and Atlantic oceans. Earlier, Capesize ships could not traverse the Suez and needed to go around the Cape of Good Hope. Recent deepening of the Suez Canal to 66 ft (20 m) permits most Capesize ships to pass through it. Capesize bulk carriers are specialised: 93% of their cargo is iron ore and coal. Some ships on the Great Lakes Waterway exceed Panamax dimensions but they are limited to use on the Great Lakes as they cannot pass through the smaller St. Lawrence Seaway to the ocean.

Very large ore carriers and very large bulk carriers are a subset of the Capesize category reserved for vessels over 200,000 DWT. Carriers of this size are almost always designed to carry iron ore and coal.

Valemax ships are a fleet of very large ore carriers (VLOC) owned or chartered by the Brazilian mining company Vale S.A. to carry iron ore from Brazil to European and Asian ports. With a capacity ranging from 380,000 to 400,000 tons deadweight, the vessels meet the Chinamax standard of ship measurements for limits on draft and beam. Valemax ships are the largest bulk carriers ever constructed, when measuring deadweight tonnage or length overall, and are among the longest ships of any type currently in service.

Case Study

Safety Management Overseas is a shipping entity associated with the Vassos P. Hajioannou family, the founder of Alassia Steamship Co. Ltd.

Vassos P. Hajioannou was born in 1933 in Pedoulas, a village on Mount Troodos in Cyprus and was one of the twelve children of Pelopidas and Maritsa Hajioannou. The family's financial means were extremely limited, therefore Vassos in 1953, at the early age of 20, immigrated to Jeddah, Saudi Arabia, in order to assist his older brother Lucas, who had already settled there, working as a shipping agent and dealer.

After many efforts and despite adversities, the business of the Hajioannou brothers grew considerably, gaining the respect of the local maritime community. Due to the nature of their work and the constant contact with the masters of vessels under their agency – mostly of Greek interests – the Hajioannou brothers accumulated knowledge and experience about the operation of shipping enterprises. This proved

MV STALO 2

25x35 inches. Oil on canvas. Courtesy Alassia New Ships Management

MV GERALDINE MANX ON THE RIVER TYNE

25x35 inches. Oil on canvas. Courtesy Ugland Bulk, Isle of Man.

highly valuable when they decided to become shipowners some years later.

Vassos Hajioannou remained in Saudi Arabia until 1962, when one of the younger Hajioannou brothers took over the family business. Lucas Hajioannou had moved to London in 1959, after getting married a year earlier. Upon moving to London, Lucas acquired the first family vessel, a 1942-built cargo steamship that was named NEDI after his wife, while its management was undertaken by the Tharros office of the Aristides Xylas family. Vassos Hajioannou, who was by then mainly dealing with the chartering of ships, acquired a minority stake on the NEDI, as well as in all other vessels that were subsequently bought by his brother. In 1961, Lucas established in London Troodos Shipping. The partnership between the two brothers continued until 1969, when Lucas and Vassos decided to part on amicable terms, as their families had grown considerably – Vassos had also got married in 1963 his compatriot Stalo, who had given birth to three of the couple's five children.

Alassia Steamship Co. Ltd., the company established by Vassos Hajioannou, began operations in May 1969 from its office in the City of London. Initially it managed two cargo sister ships acquired in 1968, the 1936-built PELOPIDAS 2 and the 1937-built MARITSA 2. Later that year, the 1939-built ELENI and KANARIS joined the fleet. All vessels were placed under the Cyprus flag and were registered in Famagusta. During that period, the Cyprus registry was growing rapidly thanks to the support of several Greek shipowners, having a significant impact in the country's economy.

Hajioannou continued expanding the Alassia fleet, acquiring in 1970 two more dry cargo ships, which were also placed under the flag of Cyprus, the STALO and the STELIOS, built in 1953 and 1955 respectively. A milestone in the company's development was the acquisition in 1972 of four dry cargo ships from the British company King Line, two built in 1952, one in 1953 and one in 1957. These vessels joined the fleet as the ELLI 2, the KANARIS, the TOULLA and the ELENI 2, respectively, all under the Cyprus flag. The timing proved ideal, as it coincided with a surge in freight rates. As a result, Alassia's balance sheet improved dramatically within a short period of time.

A year earlier, Vassos Hajioannou had relocated to Greece, establishing offices in Piraeus, which was rapidly becoming an important maritime hub. As part of his relocation he commissioned the construction of an office building to house Alassia's operations, as well as other companies.

The Turkish invasion of Cyprus in 1974 shook Hajioannou, who decided to offer land plots that he owned in Nicosia, for the setting up of refugee camps. He also donated a significant amount – disproportionately large for his financial status – to support his fellow countrymen. At the same time, all Alassia vessels were maintained under the Cyprus flag, at a time when the growth momentum of the Cyprus registry was reversed, due to the developments in the country.

Unlike his brother Lucas, who was mainly active in the tanker sector, Vassos was relatively restrained as far as his shipping investments were concerned, acquiring exclusively dry cargo ships. In 1973, he bought his first bulk carrier, a 5-year-old 40,000-dwt vessel. The STALO 2, as the ship was named, was acquired for $11 million, an unusually high price for the time's standards, which nevertheless reflected the booming freight market. The vessel was fixed for two years to a Chinese charterer, but at the time of redelivery the market had plummeted. Vassos Hajioannou faced an extremely difficult situation, having to repay a substantial loan, which was not in line with prevailing market conditions.

Nonetheless, thanks to his ingenuity, he managed to overcome this hardship. At the time, Saudi Arabia was experiencing a construction boom. Hajioannou turned to old acquaintances from his Jeddah years and managed to close a deal for the supply of about 3 million tons of cement. Combining transport and trading, he was buying cement and was supplying it to the Saudis with his own ships, thus overcoming the crisis at a profit. He often said that this deal was the result of the reputation and contacts he had built while working in Saudi Arabia and that he always made sure to maintain his reputation at any cost.

Hajioannou followed that principle when he was forced to cancel four newbuilding orders, placed in 1976 at British and Japanese shipyards. In order to avoid exchange rate risk, he had bought in advance pound sterling and Japanese yen, as the four orders were placed in local currencies. Even though he lost the deposits he had paid for the four vessels – as per the terms of the contracts – the gain from not getting delivery of overvalued assets, as well as the significant overvaluation of the yen he was holding, outweighed the loss of the deposits. Vassos Hajioannou had managed to overcome yet another obstacle, without damaging his reputation.

Taking advantage of the improved freight market in the late 1970s, Alassia completed its shift towards the bulk carrier sector, selling at a high price its general cargo fleet, while buying in 1979 two bulkers, the 1968-built PELOPIDAS and MARITSA. Two years later, Hajioannou sold the PELOPIDAS at a significant profit. His fleet now consisted of just two bulkers, something that proved a blessing during the deep crisis of the 1980s. He avoided expanding his fleet during that challenging time, with the exception of a bulk carrier acquired in 1983, which was subsequently sold in 1988 to Chinese interests at a considerable profit. In 1986, just as the market started to recover, he acquired two 9-year-old bulkers, 40,000 dwt each, at rock-bottom prices.

Prudent management during the crisis laid the foundations on which Alassia's contemporary philosophy was built, that is the provision of a first class service through a modern fleet of newly-built bulk carriers. The new generation of the family, Vassos' eldest son Polys, a naval architect, and his younger brother Nikos, had by then joined the company.

A new chapter opened in 1995 with the delivery of Alassia's first two newly-built Panamax bulk carriers from Samsung Heavy Industries Co. Ltd. in South Korea. A short while before their delivery, Vassos Hajioannou announced to his son Polys that from then on, the family's younger generation was then one to grow the company and that he would only remain as an adviser to his sons, sticking to his word even though he was only 62.

Even though he had voluntarily retired from Alassia's day-to-day operations, Hajioannou made his mark once again by deciding the company's new name. As at the time the ISM Code was about to be implemented, requiring the presence of a full management company in Greece, he suggested to name it "Safety Management" and simply add the word "Overseas".

Vassos Hajioannou passed away in 2002 leaving behind some important entrepreneurial and public benefit initiatives. However, according to his closed ones, his greatest success was the preparation of his son Polys to take over and expand the family business.

Polys Hajioannou took the helm of the company at the age of thirty-six. Within 14 years its fleet reached thirty-eight ships, most of them newly-built. In 2008 it entered in the New York Stock Exchange, with the majority holding remaining with the Hajioannou family. Meanwhile, Polys' younger brother, Nikos Hajioannou, followed in his father's footsteps by reviving Alassia through Alassia Newships Management. (courtesy of 'A Greek Shipping Miracle')

MV DESERT CALM

25x35 inches. Oil on canvas

MV PENELOPE I

*pictured at the English Bay Anchorage, Vancouver. 25x35 inche. Oil on canvas.
Courtesy Neda Maritime Agencies, Greece*

MV KRANIA IN THE COLUMBIA RIVER

30x40 inches. Oil on canvas. Courtesy Neda Maritime Agencies, Greece

MV CALYPSO LOADING AT UST LUGA

25x35 inche. Oil on canvas. Courtesy Atlantic Coal and Bulk

MV. ALEXANDRIA IN DRYDOCK

25x35 inches. Oil on canvas. Courtesy Neda Maritime Agencies, Greece

Case Study: Eddie Steamship Co. Ltd

Eddie Steamship Co. Ltd. traces its history to the island of Zhoushan off the coast of Ningbo, China, where its founder Hsu Ting-Zuo (a.k.a. Charles Eddie Hsu) was born in 1882. Growing up on an island surrounded by the sea and where operating fishing boats was the main livelihood for its inhabitants, he became familiar with seafaring at a young age, similar to many island Greek shipowners.

His father died when he was a young man from a cholera epidemic so he eventually migrated to Shanghai, the international business and financial centre of the Far East at the time, to find work. He worked at several jobs before eventually landing a position as the manager of the western restaurant at the Astor House Hotel where he was able to interact with many foreign entrepreneurs, which gave him many business ideas. One of his early businesses was the Eddie Hardware Store, where many sailors came to buy spare parts and tools for their ships. But ironically his most successful early venture was the Eddie Aerated Water Co. which produced various flavoured soda drinks. This was a thriving business for the Hsu family from the 1920's until the end of the 1940's and was managed by his eldest son Hsu Ven-Kuei (a.k.a. V.K. Eddie Hsu).

In 1922 Hsu Ting-Zuo started his first shipping venture with a fellow Zhoushan native Mr. Chu Bao-san, Chairman of the Shanghai Chamber of Commerce, and built the 1,253 gross tons S.S. Chusan, which was a passenger and general cargo vessel which traded along the coast of China. In 1927 he established his own shipping company, Eddie Steamship Co. Ltd., with the acquisition of the 1,242 tons deadweight S.S. *Hsin Yung Chuen* which was also a coastal passenger and general cargo vessel. At the outbreak of the Sino-Japanese War in 1937 when Japan occupied most of the coastal areas of China, his second son Hsu Ven-Yung transferred her to the German flag and she was renamed the S.S. *Kondor* to avoid harassment by the Japanese navy.

At the end of WWII she reverted back to the Chinese flag and was renamed S.S. *Dah Foong*. Also during the war years, two of Eddie Steamship's vessels were requisitioned by the Chinese Government, filled with sand and gravel, and sunk in the Yangtze River near Jiangyin to block the Japanese navy from going up the river.

Hsu Ting-Zuo passed away in 1941 at the rather young age of fifty-nine and the shipping side of his enterprises came under the management of the youngest of his three sons, Wen-Hwa Eddie Hsu (a.k.a. W.H. Eddie Hsu). At the end of WWII China experienced a brief period of economic boom and the company acquired its first ocean going vessel the 3,500 tons deadweight SS *Eddie* in November 1946 and the 1,200 tons deadweight SS *Hsiang Li* in March 1947, both built in the UK. But soon China descended into civil war between the ruling Kuomingtang and the Communists. The SS *Hsiang Li* was bombed and sunk in the Yangtze River in mid-1949 and soon thereafter a Communist victory seemed imminent, so the company relocated from Shanghai to Taipei on the island of Taiwan with just the SS *Eddie* sailing to the port of Keelung.

Although this was a turbulent time for the company, with the outbreak of the Korean War in mid-1950, demand for shipping increased and freight rates firmed up which gave the company a respite. But with the unstable environment it was difficult to get financing to grow the company's fleet, and it was at this time that W.H. Eddie Hsu met an old friend of his father, British businessman George Marden of Wheelock Marden & Co. who had relocated from Shanghai to Hong Kong. With the assistance of Wheelock Marden in getting loans in Hong Kong, the company's fleet expanded quickly. Two main sources of tonnage for the company was Ellerman Line of the UK

SS. EDDIE PICTURED AT SHANGHAI

25x35 inches. Oil on canvas. Courtesy Eddie Steamship Co.

and US war surplus Liberty and T2 ships.

The venerable British shipping company Ellerman Line, with over 100 years of history, had a huge fleet under its flag. But with the gradual decline of the British Empire, especially the independence of India, they decided to pare down the fleet. Many of these ships were acquired by Eddie Steamship including the SS *City of Lichfield* (renamed the *Camerona*), SS *City of Bristol* (renamed *Tunglee*), SS *City of Madras* (renamed *Weilee*), SS *City of Durham* (renamed *Yonlee*), SS *City of Carlisle* (renamed *Jeannie*), SS *City of Lucknow* (renamed *Lisboa*) and the SS *City of Coventry* (renamed *Ingrid*). These were all general cargo vessels but as was common in that era, they also carried upwards of twenty passengers. When these ships were eventually demolished in Kaohsiung in the 1960's, some of the crockery and silverware was removed to the company's Taipei office and are still displayed in the conference room.

The Liberty class of ships were 10,000 deadweight general cargo ships built by the U.S., British and Canadian governments on a mass production line scale to a unified blueprint to counter the decimation of the allied merchant fleet by German submarines during WWII. Between 1942 to 1945 over 2700 of these ships were built at the incredible average building time of just 42 days each. At the end of the war, most were sold as war surplus and for many later day Greek and Chinese shipping tycoons, these Liberty ships formed the backbone of their rise and are remembered fondly. During the 1950's and 1960's Eddie Steamship owner a total of sixteen such Liberty vessels.

The "T2" class of ships were the oil tanker counterpart to the Liberty ships. During the war years over 500 were built to the same master blueprint. After the war the Greek shipping legend Stavros Niarchos purchased many of these T2 vessels and traded them as tankers in the 1940's and '50's. In the late 1950's Niarchos lengthened many of these vessel by adding a new mid-ship section and converted them to dry bulk carriers. Some were fitted with cargo gears and some were gearless. During the 1960's the Eddie Steamship group purchased ten such converted T2 vessels from the Niarchos group and traded them well into the 1970's carrying sugar *(cont on page 102)*

SS HSIANG LI AT SHANGHAI

*The general cargo carrier SS **Hsiang Li** of 1296 long tons deadweight, length overall 250.2 feet, breadth 34 feet. This vessel was operated by Eddie Steamship of Shanghai is pictured off the Shanghai Bund soon after delivery to the company in March 1947. According to Lloyd's of London, she was built in 1919 as yard number 377 at A. Roger & Company, Glasgow as the SS **Lyminge** for Constants Limited of London. **Hsiang Li** was bombed and sunk in the Yangtze River in 1949. During her two years of service with the company she would have carried general cargoes between Tianjin, Shanghai, Ningbo, Keelung and Guangzhou along the China Coast*

25x35 inches. Oil on canvas. Courtesy Eddie Steamship.

SS. BARBARA IN NEW YORK HARBOUR

The bulk carrier SS **Barbara** *of 22,959 tons deadweight, length overall 555.9 feet and breadth 75.2 feet was operated by Eddie Steamship and is pictured passing Manhattan Island, New York City, circa 1966 having just discharged her cargo of sugar at the Pepsi Cola terminal at Yonkers, NY and sailing down the Hudson River.*

The vessel was originally built as the SS **Owyhee** *at the Kaiser Company Swan Island shipyard in Portland Oregon in 1943 as an oil tanker by the US Maritime Commission on a mass production basis (over 500 exact sisterships were built) to keep the allies supplied during World War II. They were commonly referred to as 'T2 Tankers' and were a counterpart to the 'Liberty' general cargo ships, also mass-produced during WW II. After the war most were sold as war surplus and this vessel was purchased by the Greek shipowner Stavros S. Niarchos in 1948 and continued trading as an oil tanker under the name SS* **World Treaty**.

In 1961 the Niarchos group undertook a major conversion of the vessel at the Hellenic Shipyards Co. in Skaramanga, Greece, fabricating a new mid-ship section, cargo holds and derricks making the ship into a bulk carrier. After conversion she was 6,346 tons deadweight bigger and 33 feet longer and was re-christened SS **World Charity**.

In 1966 Eddie Steamship purchased her and renamed her SS **Barbara** *(one of ten sisterships acquired). Her main trading routes were to carry bulk sugar from the Philippines to the US East Coast including the Ports of New York, Philadelphia and Charleston. Afterwards she would load soybeans, maize or wheat from the US Gulf coast for discharge at the ports of Keelung and Kaohsiung in Taiwan. The ship was sold for demolition in Kaohsiung in 1975.*

25x35 inches. Oil on canvas. Courtessy Eddie Steamship

SS LUCINA

This vessel was one of the famous 'Liberty' series of cargo ships built during World War II. In the early 1940's the British were in danger of capitulation not due to losses on the battlefield, but due to the fact that German submarines were relentlessly sinking British Merchant ships and Britain was about to have it supply lines cut.

*The British and American governments devised a plan to mass produce cargo ships to a single design to be built mainly in the US. The plan was to build these ships faster than the Germans could sink them. At the peak of production these 'Liberty' ships were being built at the amazing speed of about 40 days each. In the case of the **Lucina** (original name **Samnegros**) her keel was laid on 11 May 1944 and she was delivered on the 22nd June 1944 for a total construction time of just 42 days. A total of 2,751 'Liberty' ships were built during the war and after the war most were sold as war surplus to merchant shipping companies.*

*Eddie Steamship acquired the **Lucina** in 1959 and operated the vessel until 1967 when she was demolished at Kaohsiung. One of her frequent trades was to carry sugar and tea from Taiwan to Iran and then proceed to Casablanca, Morocco to load phosphate back to Taiwan.*

This historical painting features the vessel passing the southern Pillars of Hercules mountains on the coast of Morocco.
25x35 inches. Oil on canvas. Courtesty Eddie Steamship

MV EMERALD TRANSPORTER

*The Ore Carrier MV **Emerald Transporter** of 183,572 metric tons deadweight, 312 metres length overall and 47.5 metres breadth. This vessel was operated by Eddie Steamship Co. Ltd. of Taipei in the 1980's.*

*In 1977, as part of the Republic of China's Ten Major Infrastructure Projects, China Steel Corp. was inaugurated in Kaohsiung, Taiwan, and Eddie Steamship secured the first contract of affreightment to carry the large steel mill's iron ore import requirements. Thus, for the first time Eddie Steamship entered the ultra-large "capesize" bulk carrier sector to move over 120,000 metric tons of iron ore per shipment from Australia, South Africa and Brazil. In the late 1970's and 1980's the company acquired a fleet of these capesize bulk carriers including the MV **Emerald Transporter** which was the largest vessel ever registered under the ROC flag at the time.*

*The painting features the vessel passing the sandstone tidal pools at the entrance of Port Hedland, Australia, with the channel markers and light posts visible on a bright sunny day, which is the typical weather condition in northwest Australia. In the background are the Eddie Steamship Group's 169,000 metric tons deadweight sisterships **Crystal Transporter** (formerly MV **English Bridge**) and MV **Iron Transporter** (formerly MV **Tyne Bridge**).*

*These are two of the six "Bridge" class Ore/Bulk/Oil carriers built during the 1970's at the Swan Hunter Shipyard on the River Tyne in the UK. In fact, during the 1980's and 1990's Eddie Steamship owned and operated four of the six sisterships having also had the MV **Ocean Sovereign** (formerly MV **Furness Bridge**) and the MV **Ocean Mandarin** (formerly MV **Sir Alexander Glen**) in its fleet. They are pictured at anchor awaiting their turn to load.*

25x35 inches. Oil on canvas. Courtesy Eddie Steamship

MV CONQUEROR

The painting features the vessel off Hon Gai Port near Halong Bay in Northern Vietnam loading coal from barges on a clear evening with a star filled sky. The coal will be destined for Guangzhou, China. In the background are some of the spectacular limestone islets, cliffs and grottos the Halong Bay area is famous for.

The painting was commissioned for an exhibition at the International Maritime Organisation headquarters in London in September 2011

30x40 inches. Oil on canvas. Courtesy Eddie Steamship

MV HEROIC

*The bulk carrier MV **Heroic** 56,720 metric tons deadweight, 189.99 metres length overall and 32.26 metres breadth. This vessel is the second of a pair built at Zengzhou Shipbuilding yard located in Dinghai, Zhoushan Island, China for Courage Marine.*

This painting features the vessel departing on her maiden voyage in February 2012 passing Mount Putuo, a holy Buddhist pilgrimage site on the Zhoushan Archipelago. In the distance on top of the mountain is the Statue of Guan Yin, the Goddess of Mercy looking out towards the East China Sea. Chinese seamen regard her as the guardian of smooth sea voyages.

The painting was commissioned by Courage Marine Chairman Chih-Chien Hsu to commemorate the christening of the vessel at his family's ancestral home of Dinghai, Zhoushan, where they started in the shipping business in 1927.

25x35 inches. Oil on canvas. Courtesy Eddie Steamship

MV OCEAN CONQUEROR

The "ultramax" type bulk carrier MV **Ocean Conqueror** of 63,362 metric tons deadweight, length overall 199.90 metres, breadth 32.26 metres, draft 13.30 metres.

This vessel was commissioned by the Eddie Steamship Group of Taipei and built at the China Merchant Heavy Industries Shipyard in Haimen, Jiangsu Province, China, and christened on 26th September 2018. Eddie Steamship has had a long relationship with the China Merchant Steam Navigation Group (founded in 1872) going back to the 1930's in Shanghai and later in the 1960's and 1970's with China Merchant Steam Navigation of Taiwan. It was fortuitous for the two groups to work together again on this project in the 21st century.

This painting features the vessel on her maiden voyage departing from Haimen to Indonesia while passing the Penghu Islands Archipelago in the Taiwan Straits. Several of the islands in this chain are famous for their unique basalt stone columns along the coast, which you can see in the background, formed when molten lava came into contact with the cool ocean water millions of years ago. This painting was commissioned for Christmas of 2018.

25x35 inches. Oil on canvas. Eddie Steamship

MV. PANAMAX UNIVERSE

The bulk carrier MV. **Panamax Universe** *of 79,393 metric tons deadweight, 229 metres length overall and 32.26 metres breadth. This vessel operated by Eddie Steamship was built at Jinhai Heavy Industries Shipyard in Zhoushan, China and delivered in April 2012.*

The painting depicts the vessel passing the Makassar Strait, Indonesia after having loaded a cargo of coal at the port of Tanjungbara for delivery to Taiwan Power Company's terminal at Taichung Port Taiwan. This is one of the regular trades for the vessel. In the background is the Dipterocaraceae lowland tropical rainforest of Kutai National Park.

25x35 inches. Oil on canvas. Courtesty Eddie Steamship

(from page 94) from the Philippines to the US East Coast and then loading grain in the US Gulf Coast back to Taiwan.

In the early 1960's Ven-Kuei Eddie Hsu relocated to Hong Kong and established Oak Steamship Co. Ltd. and became an active member of the maritime community there. In 2002 Oak Maritime (Hong Kong) Inc. Ltd. diversified into the oil tanker sector and their first two VLCC's were aptly named the MT *Charles Eddie* and the MT *Kondor*.

With the economy of Taiwan (and Japan, South Korea and other East Asian countries) growing at double digit rates in the 1960' and 1970's, Eddie Steamship's rapidly growing fleet was well positioned to carry it's booming import of raw materials and the export of finished goods. At this time Eddie Steamship also embarked on a major newbuilding programme with its first new vessel, the MV *Mandarin* (42,000mt DWT) being built at Mitsubishi Heavy Industries in Japan in 1967, the 40th anniversary of the company's founding. Further newbuilding's followed at MHI and also Hitachi Zosen. In 1976 the Eddie Group supported the Taiwan government's Ten Major Infrastructure Projects by becoming the largest private shareholder in the China Shipbuilding Corp. and ordering a total of fifteen newbuilds from its Keelung and Kaohsiung shipyards throughout the 1970's and 1980's.

But in the 1970's the world of shipping was going through a major change. With the advent of containerisation of shipping, general cargo ships became obsolete and the company gradually phased them out and became an exclusively bulk carrier fleet. Two other developments in the 1970's resulted in the ships of the Eddie Group becoming much bigger in deadweight tonnage size. First, China Steel Corp., another

of the Ten Major Infrastructure Projects in Taiwan, was inaugurated in 1977. Eddie Steamship secured the first contract of affreightment (COA) to carry the large iron ore requirements of the steel mill, which needed to be shipped on capesized bulk carriers of over 100,000 tons deadweight each. Second was the two world oil crises during that period which lead Taiwan Power Company to diversify its energy sources with the large importation of coal which needed to be carried on Panamax sized bulk carriers. By the early 1980's although the number of ships in the company's fleet remained about 50, its total deadweight tons increased from about 1 million metric tons to well over 4 million metric tons.

The mid-1980's proved to be an extremely challenging time for the international maritime industry and Eddie Steamship was also caught up in the gathering storm. A combination of rapid fleet growth due to advances in shipbuilding technology, a slowdown in the world economy due to the two oil crises, and extremely high US dollar interest rates (the currency of international ship finance) combined to make the worst peacetime crisis in shipping. Numerous shipping groups faced financial collapse and Eddie Steamship was no exception. The company's U.S., European and Japanese banks foreclosed on most of the company's fleet. Ironically with its much-reduced fleet the company's financial position actually stabilised because the remaining vessels were concentrated in carrying cargoes of the few profitable older COA's and the company was able to gradually repay its creditors. But the crisis took a heavy toll on the health of W.H. Eddie Hsu and he passed away in 1987 but the company's operation continued uninterrupted under the guidance of four of his six children, two sons and two daughter, into the 1990's.

In 1999 the youngest son, Chih-Chien Hsu, formed a joint venture company, Courage Marine Group Ltd., together with several partners in Taiwan's maritime industry and in 2005 listed on the Singapore Stock Exchange. In 2011 the company did a second listing in the Hong Kong Stock Exchange. Due to the economic liberalisation in mainland China, its economy took off during the first decade of the 21st century and because of its vast scale the maritime industry enjoyed an unprecedented boom. Courage Marine benefited from this buoyant market and was repeatedly ranked as one of the best performing listed shipping companies in the world. In 2011 C.C. Hsu returned to his family's ancestral home of Zhoushan, which had become a major shipbuilding centre in China, to place newbuilding orders on behalf of Courage Marine for two 57,000mt deadweight supramax bulk carriers, the MV *Zorina* and the MV *Heroic*. In 2012 C.C. Hsu's private Eddie Steamship purchased a newbuilding resale 79,600mt deadweight kamsarmax bulk carrier from another Zhoushan shipyard, Jinhai Heavy Industries which was named the MV *Panamax Universe*.

In 2017 Eddie Steamship commemorated its 90th anniversary but the oldest continuing shipping company in Chinese history is the state-owned China Merchant Steam Navigation Co. Ltd. which was founded in 1872 during the Qing Dynasty. During the Republic of China era in mainland China from the 1920's to the end of the 1940's Eddie Steamship always maintained close ties its big brother. After the China Merchant fleet was split into the mainland branch and the Taiwan branch after the civil war, Eddie Steamship continued to maintain very close ties with the Taiwan branch as cargoes from all state-owned corporations were distributed via China Merchant Steam Navigation. Therefore, it was fortuitous that in 2018 the Eddie Steamship Group took delivery of a newbuilding 64,000mt deadweight ultramax class bulk carrier, the MV *Ocean Conqueror*, built at China Merchant Heavy Industries, Jiangsu Province, a subsidiary of China Merchant Group of Shanghai. The relationship had come full circle.

TANKERS
POWERING THE WORLD

An oil tanker, also known as a petroleum tanker, is a ship designed for the bulk transport of oil or its products. There are two basic types of oil tankers: crude tankers and product tankers. Crude tankers move large quantities of unrefined crude oil from its point of extraction to refineries. Product tankers, generally much smaller, are designed to move refined products from refineries to points near consuming markets. For example, moving gasoline from refineries in Europe to consumer markets in Nigeria and other West African nations.

Oil tankers are often classified by their size as well as their occupation. The size classes range from inland or coastal tankers of a few thousand metric tons of deadweight (DWT) to the mammoth ultra-large crude carriers (ULCCs) of 550,000 DWT. Tankers move approximately 2,000,000,000 metric tons (2.2×109 short tons) of oil every year. Second only to pipelines in terms of efficiency, the average cost of oil transport by tanker amounts to only two or three United States cents per 1 US gallon (3.8 L).

The modern oil tanker was developed in the period from 1877 to 1885.[10] In 1876, Ludvig and Robert Nobel, brothers of Alfred Nobel, founded Branobel (short for Brothers Nobel) in Baku, Azerbaijan. It was, during the late 19th century, one of the largest oil companies in the world.

Ludvig was a pioneer in the development of early oil tankers. He first experimented with carrying oil in bulk on single-hulled barges. Turning his attention to self-propelled tankships, he faced a number of challenges. A primary concern was to keep the cargo and fumes well away from the engine room to avoid fires. Other challenges included allowing for the cargo to expand and contract due to temperature changes and providing a method to ventilate the tanks.

The first successful oil tanker was *Zoroaster,* which carried its 242 long tons of kerosene cargo in two iron tanks joined by pipes. One tank was forward of the midships engine room and the other was aft. The ship also featured a set of 21 vertical watertight compartments for extra buoyancy. The ship had a length overall of 184 feet (56 m), a beam of 27 feet (8.2 m), and a draft of 9 feet.

In 1883, oil tanker design took a large step forward. Working for the Nobel company, British engineer Colonel Henry F. Swan designed a set of three Nobel tankers. Instead of one or two large holds, Swan's design used several holds which spanned the width, or beam, of the ship. These holds were further subdivided into port and starboard sections by a longitudinal bulkhead. Earlier designs suffered from stability problems caused by the free surface effect, where oil sloshing from side to side could cause a ship to capsize. But this approach of dividing the ship's storage space into smaller tanks virtually eliminated free surface problems. This approach, almost universal today, was first used by Swan in the Nobel tankers Blesk, Lumen, and Lux.

The 1880s also saw the beginnings of the Asian oil trade. The idea that led to moving Russian oil to the Far East via the Suez Canal was the brainchild of two

MT JAHRE VIKING AT SEA
30x40 inches. Oil on canvas. Courtesy Mr R. Grool

men: importer Marcus Samuel and shipowner/broker Fred Lane. Prior bids to move oil through the canal had been rejected by the Suez Canal Company as being too risky. Samuel approached the problem a different way by asking the company for the specifications of a tanker it would allow through the canal.

Armed with the canal company's specifications, Samuel ordered three tankers from William Gray & Company in northern England. Named Murex, Conch and Clam, each had a capacity of 5,010 long tons of deadweight. These three ships were the first tankers of the Tank Syndicate, forerunner of today's Royal Dutch Shell company.

With facilities prepared in Jakarta, Singapore, Bangkok, Saigon, Hong Kong, Shanghai, and Kobe, the fledgling Shell company was ready to become Standard Oil's first challenger in the Asian market. On August 24, 1892, Murex became the first tanker to pass through the Suez Canal. By the time Shell merged with Royal Dutch Petroleum in 1907, the company had 34 steam-driven oil tankers, compared to Standard Oil's four case-oil steamers and sixteen sailing tankers.

The supertanker era.

Until 1956, tankers were designed to be able to navigate the Suez Canal. This size restriction became much less of a priority after the closing of the canal during the Suez Crisis of 1956. Forced to move oil around the Cape of Good Hope, shipowners realised that bigger tankers were the key to more efficient transport. While a typical T2

AL DAFNA

The Ras Gas Q-Max LNG carrier is pictured at Sabine Pass LNG Terminal.
25x35 inches. Oil on canvas. Courtesy Ras Gas.

tanker of the World War II era was 532 feet (162 m) long and had a capacity of 16,500 DWT, the ultra-large crude carriers (ULCC) built in the 1970s were over 1,300 feet (400 m) long and had a capacity of 500,000 DWT. Several factors encouraged this growth. Hostilities in the Middle East which interrupted traffic through the Suez Canal contributed, as did nationalisation of Middle East oil refineries. Fierce competition among shipowners also played a part. But apart from these considerations is a simple economic advantage: the larger an oil tanker is, the more cheaply it can move crude oil, and the better it can help meet growing demands for oil.

In 1955 the world's largest supertanker was the 47,500 DWT: SS *Spyros Niarchos* launched that year by Vickers Armstrong's Shipbuilders Ltd in England for Stavros Niarchos.

In 1958 United States shipping magnate Daniel K. Ludwig broke the record of 100,000 long tons of heavy displacement. His Universe Apollo displaced 104,500 long tons, a 23% increase from the previous record-holder, Universe Leader which also belonged to Ludwig.

The world's largest supertanker was built in 1979 at the Oppama shipyard by Sumitomo Heavy Industries, Ltd., named *Seawise Giant*. This ship was built with a capacity of 564,763 DWT, a length overall of 458.45 metres (1,504.1 ft) and a draft of 24.611 metres (80.74 ft). She had 46 tanks, 31,541 square metres (339,500 sq. ft) of deck, and at her full load draft, could not navigate the English Channel. *Seawise Giant* was renamed *Happy Giant* in 1989, *Jahre Viking* in 1991, and *Knock Nevis* in 2004 (when she was converted into a permanently moored storage tanker). In 2009 she was sold for the last time, renamed *Mont*, and scrapped.

As of 2011, the world's two largest working supertankers are the TI-class supertankers TI *Europe* and TI *Oceania*. These ships were built in 2002 and 2003 as *Hellespont Alhambra* and *Hellespont Tara* for the Greek Hellespont Steamship Corporation. Hellespont sold these ships to Overseas Shipholding Group and Euronav in 2004. Each of the sister ships has a capacity of over 441,500 DWT, a length overall

of 380.0 metres (1,246.7 ft) and a cargo capacity of 3,166,353 barrels (503,409,900 l). They were the first ULCCs to be double-hulled. To differentiate them from smaller ULCCs, these ships are sometimes given the V-Plus size designation.

With the exception of the pipeline, the tanker is the most cost-effective way to move oil today. Worldwide, tankers carry some 2 billion barrels annually, and the cost of transportation by tanker amounts to only US$0.02 per gallon at the pump.

Some specialised types of oil tankers have evolved including highly specialised chemical tankers designed to transport chemicals in bulk. As defined in MARPOL Annex II, chemical tanker means a ship constructed or adapted for carrying in bulk any liquid product listed in chapter seventeen of the International Bulk Chemical Code. As well as industrial chemicals and clean petroleum products, such ships also often carry other types of sensitive cargo which require a high standard of tank cleaning, such as palm oil, vegetable oils, tallow, caustic soda, and methanol.

Oceangoing chemical tankers range from 5,000 tonnes deadweight (DWT) to 35,000 DWT in size, which is smaller than the average size of other tanker types due to the specialised nature of their cargo and the size restrictions of the port terminals where they call to load and discharge.

Chemical tankers normally have a series of separate cargo tanks which are either coated with specialised coatings such as phenolic epoxy or zinc paint or made from stainless steel. The coating or cargo tank material determines what types of cargo a tank can carry for example stainless steel tanks are required for aggressive acid cargoes such as sulfuric and phosphoric acid, while 'easier' cargoes — such as vegetable oil — can be carried in epoxy coated tanks. The coating or tank material also influences how quickly tanks can be cleaned. Typically, ships with stainless steel tanks can carry a wider range of cargoes and can clean more quickly between one cargo and another, which justifies the additional cost of their construction.

Another specialist type of tanker is the LNG carrier designed for transporting liquefied natural gas (LNG). As the LNG market grows rapidly the fleet of LNG carriers continues to experience tremendous growth. The first LNG carrier Methane Pioneer (5,034 DWT) left the Calcasieu River on the Louisiana Gulf coast on 25 January 1959. Carrying the world's first ocean cargo of LNG, it sailed to the UK where the cargo was delivered. Subsequent expansion of that trade has brought on a large expansion of the fleet to today where giant LNG ships carrying up to 266,000 m3 (9,400,000 cu ft) are sailing worldwide.

The success of the specially modified C1-M-AV1-type standard ship Normarti, renamed Methane Pioneer, caused the Gas Council and Conch International Methane Ltd. to order two purpose-built LNG carriers to be constructed: Methane Princess and Methane Progress. The ships were fitted with Conch independent aluminium cargo tanks and entered the Algerian LNG trade in 1964. These ships had a capacity of 27,000 cubic metres (950,000 cu ft).

In the late 1960s, opportunity arose to export LNG from Alaska to Japan, and in 1969 that trade with TEPCO and Tokyo Gas was initiated. Two ships, Polar Alaska and Arctic Tokyo, each with a capacity of 71,500 cubic metres (2,520,000 cu ft), were built in Sweden. In the early 1970s, the US government encouraged US shipyards to build LNG carriers, and a total of 16 LNG ships were built. The late 1970s and early 1980s brought the prospect of Arctic LNG ships with several projects being studied.

With the increase in cargo capacity to approximately 143,000 cubic metres (5,000,000 cu ft), new tank designs were developed, from Moss Rosenberg to Technigaz Mark III and Gaztransport No.96.

In recent years, the size and capacity of LNG carriers has *(cont on page 110)*

SS TEXACO FLORIDA AT NEW YORK

Built in 1956 in Newport News Shipbuilding Co. USA. 20x30 inches. Oil on canvas. Courtesy American Bureau of Shipping

MV BRITISH QUEEN

Pictured at Port Said. 30x40 inches. Oil on canvas. Courtesy Mr. D Kenwright collection

MV. BRITISH DRAGOON

pictured in the Scottish Lochs. 20x30 inches. Oil on canvas. Private collection

MT IONIC ANASSA

Under construction at the Namura Shipyard, Japan. 30x40 inches. Oil on canvas.
Courtesy Ionic Ship Management

UNDER A STARRY SKY – HELLESPONT PROVIDENCE

A detailed study of the accommodation of a modern Aframax tanker.
25x35 inches. Oil on canvas. Private Collection.

LNG TAURUS CONDUCTING SHIP TO SHIP TRANSFER (STS) WITH THE AKEBONO MARU

25x35 inches. Oil on canvas. Courtesy Mitsui OSK LNG

VLADIMIR RUSANOV PICTURED LEAVING THE RUSSIAN ARCTIC IN ICE

In 2017, Daewoo Shipbuilding & Marine Engineering delivered the Vladimir Rusanov, an icebreaking LNG tanker of 80,200 deadweight tons. Her capacity of 172,600 m3 (6,100,000 cu ft) is the consumption of Sweden for a month. She completed her first revenue voyage from Norway via the Northern Sea Route in the Arctic Ocean to South Korea. The shipyard has fourteen more sister ships on order. 25x35 inches. Oil on canvas. Courtesy MOL LNG.

MT MARI JONE

Pictured in New Plymouth New Zealand. 25x35 inches. Oil on canvas.
Courtesy Thome Ship Management Singapore.

MT NAVIGATOR PLUTO

pictured at Dusk loading ethylene in South America at dusk. 35x45 inches. Oil on canvas.
Courtesy Navigator Gas.

THE VLCC NEPTUNE GLORY

30x40 inches. Oil on canvas. Courtesy Neptune Glory GmbH & Co, Tankschiff KG.

MT. MARAN ARES AT SINGAPORE

25x35 inches. Oil on canvas. Courtesy SeaRiver Inc.

(from page 104) increased greatly. Since 2005, Qatargas has pioneered the development of two new classes of LNG carriers, referred to as Q-Flex and Q-Max. Each ship has a cargo capacity of between 210,000 and 266,000 cubic metres (7,400,000 and 9,400,000 cu ft) and is equipped with a re-liquefaction plant.

Case Study – Neda Maritime Agency

Since as early as the 18th century many generations of the founding family, based on the Ionian island of Cephalonia, had owned and operated sailing vessels which traded throughout the Adriatic, Mediterranean and Black Sea, and as far afield as Western Europe.

In those earlier times few owners-maintained companies or offices ashore, but during the 1880's it became clear that a more formal management system would be required, and thus Neda Maritime Agency was formed, with the founding family purchasing its first steam ship in 1888, the SS. *Eleni Mila*. In 1892 an office was opened in Cardiff, and 3 years later an office in London. At that time, The Company was listed as operating the largest Greek fleet by tonnage. An original member of the Union of Greek Ship Owners, The Company also provided its first President by election for its first 8 years.

In 1896 the Company placed its first order in the UK for the construction of a steamship, the SS. *Fotis* thus starting a tradition of operating very modern vessels, usually newbuildings constructed to its own exacting specifications.

During WW1 the Company suffered the loss of four vessels due to enemy action. Subsequently, during the inter-war period, the Company's operations moved to Athens but returned to London due to the enemy occupation of Greece during WW2. Neda's representative was responsible for all Greek-owned vessels at the UK Ministry of Transport throughout the War years.

Neda Maritime Agency suffered further heavy losses of tonnage during WW2. At the end of hostilities, unlike many other Greek companies which opted to purchase Liberty ships, Neda purchased its first tanker (a T2 renamed *Kate NL*), thus becoming the first Greek company to operate tankers. Since then, Neda has maintained an unbroken history of operating tanker vessels alongside its dry cargo fleet.

During the 1950's, 1960's and 1970's, Neda Maritime Agency resumed its newbuilding programme, ordering a large number of tankers of increasing sizes over that time. Neda was one of the first foreign companies to place an order in Japan (m/t *Anatzouletta* of 16,000 dwt in 1952 from Hitachi Zosen, then known as Osaka Iron Works). This was the start of a long and fruitful relationship between Neda Maritime and Hitachi Zosen (now Universal Shipbuilding) which in 2000 celebrated the 50th year of co-operation between the two companies, with Neda taking delivery of Hitachi Zosen's 100th Panamax bulk carrier (m/v *Spartia* of 75,000 dwt).

In 1974 the Company took delivery of its first Very Large Crude Carrier, the m/t *Sanko Stresa*, from the HDW Shipyard of Kiel, Germany. Later, in the early 1980's, Neda was one of the pioneers of the Long-Range Products Tanker market, operating 4 LR1 vessels during that decade, two of which were also constructed at Hitachi Zosen.

A historic step was taken in 1990, when Neda ordered the world's first double hull VLCC, the m/t *AROSA*. Neda worked closely with Hitachi Zosen and Lloyd's

MT AROSA

Pictured departing the Hyundai Shipyard, Ulsan South Korea. 25x35 inches. Oil on canvas. Courtesy of Neda Maritime Agency.

MT SERIANA AT ULSAN, SOUTH KOREA

25x35 inches. Oil on canvas. Courtesy Neda Maritime Agency

MV IANTHE OFF GIBRALTAR 'AWAITING ORDERS'

Built in 1953 by Haverton Hill, she was completed as **Merchant Baron** *for the Drake Shipping Company and reflagged to Liberia, renamed* **IANTHE** *in 1963.*
25x35 inches oil on canvas. Private collection

MT SILVAPLANA BERTHING IN JAPAN

25x35 inche.s Oil on canvas. Courtesy Neda Maritime

MT AQUILLA LOADING FROM BUOY OFF RAS LAFFAN

25x35 inches. Oil on canvas. Courtesy Neda Maritime Agencies

MT CHARLES EDDIE THE RIVER SEINE

Built by Daewoo Shipbuilding and Engineering Co. Okpo, South Korea, 2002.
25x35 inches. Oil on canvas. Courtesy Oak Maritime Hong Kong

Register of Shipping to develop the design of the vessel from scratch, there being no detailed rules and regulations yet developed at that time for the design and construction of very large double hull vessels. The vessel was delivered to Neda Maritime Agency in February of 1993, making her the first double hull VLCC in the World to trade commercially. It is a testament to the foresight and high standards of Neda's technical design team that the numerous dimensional and design decisions made by Neda, in close co-operation with Lloyd's Register, in the planning and construction of m/t *AROSA* were adopted as the industry standard for such vessels.

Within the first decade of the 21st century, the Neda fleet has expanded due to increased world cargo demand to more than double its numbers of previous decades, and a fourfold increase in its tonnage, with over 70 sale and purchase transactions having been made during this period, including taking delivery of sixteen newbuilding's. At the start of 2012 the Neda fleet numbered twenty-seven vessels, tankers and bulk carriers, of which five are VLCCs and eight are Capesize bulk carriers, totalling a deadweight tonnage of almost 4.5 million metric tonnes.

A continuing newbuilding programme for delivery of vessels in the coming years seeks to maintain the Company's tradition and practice of offering our clients a modern, high quality fleet, with exceptional standards of technical maintenance and operational professionalism.

Since the purchase of that first steam ship, the Company is now celebrating almost 140 years in the ship management business, making Neda Maritime one of the oldest Greek shipping companies in existence and still under the Presidency of a direct descendant of the founding family.

Case Study - The Oak Maritime Group

Established in 1961 in Hong Kong, the Oak Maritime Group is one of the most solid medium size family controlled shipping companies in Asia with extensive interests in dry cargo bulk carriers and crude oil tankers.

The Group has grown steadily and currently associates with the following companies:

1. Sincere Navigation Corporation (SNC), Taiwan (established in 1968, SNC publicly listed on the Taiwan Stock Exchange in 1989, stock code 2605.TT)
2. Oak Maritime (Canada) Inc., Vancouver (established in 1993)
3. Oak Maritime (UK) Ltd., London (established in 1998)
4. Haihu Maritime Service (Shanghai) Co., Ltd., Shanghai (established in 2003)
5. Oak Maritime (Singapore) Pte. Ltd., Singapore (established in 2016)

With offices in Taipei, Vancouver, London, Shanghai and Singapore, the Group's general management is coordinated through its Hong Kong headquarter, Oak Maritime (Hong Kong) Inc. Limited.

The Group's fully integrated services include technical management, crew management, chartering, post fixture operations, fleet insurance, accounting services, ship-brokering, and newbuilding projects supervision and management. These various roles allow the Group to provide a seamless, round-the-clock global shipping market coverage and provide its clients with unrivalled performance competency in an increasingly challenging shipping environment.

Over the past 50 plus years, the Group has developed a young, well-maintained fleet to safely carry and deliver cargoes to its customers, thus building a solid reputation for high standard of service with an impeccable track record.

The History

The Hsu family's history in shipping can be traced back to the 1920s in Shanghai when the Group's founding father, Mr. Charles Eddie Hsu established Eddie Steamship Co. Ltd. His son, the late Mr. V. K. Eddie Hsu, established the family's first shipping presence in Taiwan in 1960.

Oak Steamship Company Limited was established in February 1961 in Hong Kong by the late Mr. V. K. Eddie Hsu, father of the present Chairman Mr. Steve G. K. Hsu. In 1994, Oak Maritime (Hong Kong) Inc. Limited was established and since then has become the hub of the various Hsu-family controlled or affiliated entities, including the Oak Group Fleet.

THE VERY LARGE ORE CARRIER TIEN SHAN

Pictured on sea-trails. 30x40 inches. Oil on canvas. Courtesy Oak Maritime, Hong Kong.

CRUISING
A BOOMING MARKET

VIKING STAR

painted on-board during her Maiden Voyage from Istanbul to Venice – pictured here on arrival at Venice. 25x35 inches. Oil on canvas. Courtesy Viking Cruises

A cruise ship is a passenger ship used for pleasure voyages when the voyage itself, the ship's amenities, and sometimes the different destinations along the way (i.e., ports of call), form part of the passengers' experience. Transportation is not the only purpose of cruising, particularly on cruises that return passengers to their originating port. On "cruises to nowhere" or "nowhere voyages", cruise ships make 2-to-3-night round trips without any ports of call.

In contrast, dedicated transport-oriented ocean liners do "line voyages" and typically transport passengers from one point to another, rather than on round trips. Traditionally, shipping lines build liners for the transoceanic trade to a higher standard than that of a typical cruise ship, including higher freeboard and stronger plating to withstand rough seas and adverse conditions encountered in the open ocean, such as the North Atlantic. Ocean liners also usually have larger capacities for fuel, food, and other stores for consumption on long voyages, compared to dedicated cruise ships, but few ocean liners remain in existence - note the preserved liners and *Queen Mary 2*, which makes scheduled North Atlantic voyages.

Although often luxurious, ocean liners had characteristics that made them unsuitable for cruising, such as high fuel consumption, deep draughts that prevented their entering shallow ports, enclosed weatherproof decks inappropriate for tropical weather, and cabins designed to maximise passenger numbers rather than comfort (such as a high proportion of windowless suites). The gradual evolution of passenger ship design from ocean liners to cruise ships has seen passenger cabins shifted from inside the hull to the superstructure and provided with private verandas. Modern cruise ships, while sacrificing some qualities of seaworthiness, have added amenities to cater to water tourists, and recent vessels have been described as "balcony-laden floating condominiums".

The distinction between ocean liners and cruise ships has blurred, particularly with respect to deployment, although differences in construction remain. Larger cruise ships have also engaged in longer trips, such as transoceanic voyages which may not return to the same port for months (longer round trips). Some former ocean liners operate as cruise ships, such as Marco Polo, although this number is diminishing. The only dedicated transatlantic ocean liner in operation as a liner As of December 2013 is *Queen Mary 2* of the Cunard Line. She also has the amenities of contemporary cruise ships and sees significant service on cruises

Cruising has become a major part of the tourism industry, accounting for US$42.4 billion, with over 19 million passengers carried worldwide as of 2018. The industry's rapid growth has seen nine or more newly-built ships catering to a North American clientele added every year since 2001, as well as others servicing European clientele

Case Study - Ocean Monarch

Ocean Monarch was built by Vickers-Armstrongs Ltd, Walker at a cost of £2,500,000. She was yard number 119, and was launched on 27 July 1950, with completion in March 1951. She was the first post-war-built ship designed especially for the American cruise market. *Ocean Monarch* was awarded a gold medal by the American Institute for Designing for her "outstanding beauty and unusual design features of a cruise ship".

Ocean Monarch was used on the New York - Bermuda route. As well as conveying passengers she was used to supply fresh drinking water to the island. She served with Furness Withy via subsidiary Furness Bermuda Line until 1966. On 22 September she was laid up in the River Fal, Cornwall. In 1967, she was sold to Navigation Maritime Bulgare and renamed *Varna*. Operated by Balkantourist, Varna, she was used on cruises from Montreal, Quebec, Canada. *Varna* was laid up in 1970 at Perama, Greece. In 1973, Varna was chartered by Sovereign Cruises, but only made two voyages with them. She was then laid up again. Her name was changed to Venus in 1977, and Riviera in 1978. In 1979, she was refurbished for use by Trans-Tirreno Express. She was chartered by SUR-Seereisen, Germany, who *(cont on page 116)*

MS MARINA IN FRENCH POLYNESIA
20x30 inches. Oil on canvas. Private collection

SS BRITANIS

The 1932 ship pictured in the Aegean. 25x18 inches. Oil on canvas. Private collection

SS LURLINE SAN FRANCISCO

20x16 inches. Oil on canvas. Courtesy Snowbow Productions (2000) Ltd

MS FINNMARKEN OFF THE COAST OF NORWAY

20x16 inches. Oil on canvas. Courtesy U. Hintermeister.

MV. COSTA ATLANTICA AT FLAM, NORWAY

30x40 inches. Oil on canvas. Courtesy Carnival Corporation, Miami.

(from page 113) announced a series of Mediterranean cruises to take place in summer 1981. Her name was changed to Reina del Mar. Before these cruises took place, the ship was renovated. On 28 May 1981, a fire broke out which completely gutted the passenger accommodation. The ship was towed out of Ambelakia, where the renovation was being carried out. The tow parted and Reina del Mar ran aground on Salamina Island. After being re-floated, she was moored near Rasa Sayang, which had also been gutted by fire. On 1 June 1981, a new fire broke out on Reina del Mar, and she was then scuttled off Kynosoura.

A personal recollection of life onboard the Ocean Monarch
by Des Kirkpatrick, Purser Ocean Monarch

I joined the *Ocean Monarch* in New York in May 1962 and remained with her until she was withdrawn from service some 4¹⁄₂ years later. She was a very happy ship and the time I spent on her was a most enjoyable experience.

The primary route for the ship was from New York to Bermuda, departing on a Saturday afternoon and arriving on Monday morning in Bermuda. On a few occasions, particularly during the winter months, the ship would take a few cruises to

MV OCEAN MONARCH APPROACHING HAMILTON, BERMUDA

25x35 inches. Oil on canvas. Courtesy Des Kirkpatrick.

SS JOIE DE VIVRE

Pictured on the River Seine, Paris. 25x35 inches. Oil on canvas. Courtesy Uniworld

SS ANTOINETTE

Pictured on the River Rhine near Oberwesel. 25x35 inches. Oil on canvas. Courtesy Uniworld

SS CATHERINE

Pictured on the Rhone River at Avignon. 25x35 inches. Oil on canvas. Courtesy Uniworld

SS RIVER QUEEN

Passing Boppard, Rhine Valley, Germany. 25x35 inches. Oil on canvas. Courtesy Uniworld

117

UNIWORLD'S SS CATHERINE

Pictured at night in Lyon. 25x35 inches. Oil on canvas. Courtesy Uniworld

the Caribbean and in the summer months she would make one or two cruises to Canada. The ship was quite small and almost yacht like and she only carried 440 passengers. St George was her usual port in Bermuda but when her consort the *Queen of Bermuda* returned to the UK for her annual refit she would then dock in Hamilton.

Sailing to Bermuda in the winter months could be uncomfortable because she did not have the regular type of stabilizers but rather "flume tanks". She could really roll and pitch.

The ship had a relatively trouble-free life although one dramatic incident happened shortly before arriving in Bermuda on Christmas Eve when we had a rather bad fire in the engine room and although we were practically in sight of Bermuda, we limped into port hours late. On returning to New York the next trip was cancelled and we had to go to the shipyard in Hoboken N.J. for repairs.

The ship was withdrawn from service in September 1966 and we sailed from New York for the last time bound for Falmouth in Cornwall where the crew were paid off and the ship was laid up and was eventually sold to Bulgaria and renamed *Varna*.

A few years later I happened to be in Palermo, and I saw this small liner arriving and realised that it was my old ship. I just had to go on board and after I had introduced myself and told them that I had spent 4^{1}/$_{2}$ years on her the first thing I was asked was where the keys to the safe in the Pursers office. They had never been able to open the safe as they could not find the key. I later learned that it had been left with one of the senior officers who had remained with the ship during the time she was laid up.

River Cruising – a whole new World of Leisure travel

River cruising has been an increasingly popular form of leisure travel in recent years. River cruises are one-week or longer, overnight passenger cruises on vessels that range in size from a small four-passenger canal barge to the largest passenger river vessel afloat, the 396-passenger *Victoria Jenna*, which operates on the Yangtze River in China.

European river cruising takes place in what is, at maximum, a 38-foot-by-410-foot vessel, dimensions dictated by the locks and bridges that the vessels must past through and under. European river cruisers generally range from between 100 and 200 passengers.

River cruises travel along many of the major rivers in the world. In Europe, the Danube River is second in length only to the Volga River in Russia. The Danube is one of the most popular rivers to cruise along, and many river cruises include the Danube as part of their itinerary.

The Main, Rhine, Moselle, Elbe, Rhone, Saone and Seine are also popular rivers in Europe for river cruising.

Elsewhere in the world, the Amazon River in Peru and Brazil, the Nile River in Egypt, the Yangtze River in China and the Mekong River in Vietnam and Cambodia are also popular river cruise destinations.

According to Douglas Ward, "A river cruise represents life in the slow lane, sailing along at a gentle pace, soaking up the scenery, with plentiful opportunities to explore riverside towns and cities en-route. It is a supremely calming experience, an antidote to the pressures of life in a fast-paced world, in surroundings that are comfortable without being fussy or pretentious, with good food and enjoyable company".

Modern river cruise vessels are essentially scaled down ocean cruise ships the main differences between river and ocean cruises are:

Riverboats are smaller than ocean liners, because of the size of the river and/or locks. Most riverboats hold between 90 and 250 passengers, but there are exceptions. The atmosphere is more intimate and friendly.

Their growing popularity is often cited that they provide a unique way of seeing a country's interior, land is always in sight and there is always something to see. Better yet for some, river cruise passengers are unlikely to get motion sickness.

Over the last ten years, river cruising has become a major tourist industry in many parts of the world and is acknowledged to be the fastest growing form of 'cruising'.

Case Study – Uniworld Boutique Cruises

Uniworld Boutique River Cruise Collection is located in Los Angeles, California and the company operates a fleet of 21 river cruising cruise ships along the rivers of Europe, Russia, Egypt, and China. Uniworld Boutique River Cruise Collection, established in 1976, is a luxury river cruise company based in Los Angeles, California.

Uniworld currently operates more than 500 river cruises annually with itineraries in more than twenty countries. Its cruises range in length from a week to a month. Along with its primary operations in Western and Central Europe, the company also works in partnerships with affiliated groups in Portugal, Russia, Egypt and China.

FERRIES
THERE AND BACK AGAIN

A ferry is a merchant vessel used to carry passengers often in combination with vehicles and cargo, across a body of water. A passenger ferry with many stops, such as in Venice, Italy, is sometimes called a water bus or water taxi.

Ferries form a part of the public transport systems of many waterside cities and islands, allowing direct transit between points at a capital cost much lower than bridges or tunnels. Ship connections of much larger distances also be called ferry services, especially if they carry vehicles.

The profession of the ferryman is embodied in Greek mythology in Charon, the boatman who transported souls across the River Styx to the Underworld.

The world's largest ferries are typically those operated in Europe, with different vessels holding the record depending on whether length, gross tonnage or car vehicle capacity is the metric.

On 11 October 1811, inventor John Stevens' ship the *Juliana*, began operation as the first steam-powered ferry (service was between New York City, and Hoboken, New Jersey).

The Elwell Ferry, a cable ferry in North Carolina, travels a distance of 110 yards (100 m), shore to shore, with a travel time of five minutes.

A contender as oldest ferry in continuous operation is the Mersey Ferry from Liverpool to Birkenhead, England. In 1150, the Benedictine Priory at Birkenhead was established. The monks used to charge a small fare to row passengers across the estuary. In 1330, Edward III granted a charter to the Priory and its successors for ever: "the right of ferry there… for men, horses and goods, with leave to charge reasonable tolls". However, there may have been a short break following the Dissolution of the monasteries.

Another claimant as the oldest ferry service in continuous operation is the Rocky Hill - Glastonbury Ferry, running between the towns of Rocky Hill and Glastonbury, Connecticut. Established in 1655, the ferry has run continuously since, only ceasing operation every winter when the river freezes over. A long running salt water ferry service is the Halifax/Dartmouth ferry, running between the cities of Halifax and Dartmouth, Nova Scotia, which has run year-round since 1752, and is currently run by the region's transit authority, Metro Transit. However the Mersey Ferry predates it as the oldest salt water ferry.

By far the largest commuter ferry system in the world is the Ferries in Istanbul, Turkey, operated by DO with eighty-seven vessels serving eighty-six ports of call. Another two of the world's large ferry systems are located in the Strait of Georgia, in the Canadian province of British Columbia, and Puget Sound, in the US state of Washington. BC Ferries in British Columbia operates 36 vessels, visiting forty-seven ports of call, while Washington State Ferries owns twenty-eight vessels, travelling to twenty ports of call around Puget Sound. On the west coast of Scotland, Caledonian MacBrayne operate a network calling at fifty ports using a fleet of thirty-one vessels,

ST CLARE

*Pictured in the Solent with **Cenwulf** at Yarmouth in the distance.*
20x30 inches. Oil on canvas. Courtesy Michael Aiken

10 of which are 80m or longer. This includes a high proportion of lifeline services to island communities and as such most of the routes are heavily subsidised by the government.

Sydney Ferries in Sydney, Australia operates 31 passenger ferries in Port Jackson (Sydney Harbour), carrying 18 million passengers annually. It operates catamarans and other types of ferries on these routes, including the Circular Quay-Manly route. Between 1938 and 1974 this route operated the South Steyne, billed at the time as the largest and fastest ferry of its type. Sydney Ferries became an independent corporation owned by the government in 2004.

Some of world's busiest ferry routes include the Star Ferry in Hong Kong and the Staten Island Ferry in New York City. The ferry's single route runs 5.2 miles (8.4 km) through New York Harbour between the New York City boroughs of Manhattan and Staten Island, with ferry boats making the trip in approximately 25 minutes. The ferry operates 24 hours a day, 7 days a week, with boats leaving every 15 to 20 minutes during peak hours and every 30 minutes at other times. It is the only direct mass-transit connection between the two boroughs. Historically, the Staten Island Ferry has charged a relatively low fare compared to other modes of transit in the area; and since

1997 the route has been fare-free.

The "Barberi class" of Staten Island Ferries were built in 1981 and 1982, each boat has a crew of 15, can carry 6,000 passengers but no cars, is 310 feet (94 m) long and 69 feet 10 inches (21.29 m) wide, with a draft of 13 feet 6 inches (4.11 m), of 3,335 gross tons, with a service speed of 16 knots (30 km/h), and engines capable of 8,000 horsepower. These ships were built at the Equitable Shipyard in New Orleans, at a cost of $16.5 million each. At the time of construction, the ships' capacity was the largest of any licensed ferry in the world.

There are three main types of ferry which I have painted over the years, these are:

Roll-on/roll-off ferries (RORO) are large conventional ferries named for the ease by which vehicles can board and leave.

Cruiseferry/RoPax, a cruiseferry is a ship that combines the features of a cruise ship with a roll-on/roll-off ferry. They are also known as RoPax for their combined Roll on/Roll-Off and passenger design.

Since 1990 high speed catamarans have revolutionised ferry services, replacing hovercraft, hydrofoils and conventional monohull ferries. In the 1990s there were a variety of builders, but the industry has consolidated to two builders of large vehicular ferries between 60 and 120 metres. Incat of Hobart, Tasmania favours a Wave-piercing hull to deliver a smooth ride, while Austal of Perth, Western Australia builds ships based on SWATH designs. Both these companies also compete in the smaller river ferry industry with several other ship builders.

Stena Line once operated the largest catamarans in the world, the Stena HSS class, between the United Kingdom and Ireland. These waterjet-powered vessels, displaced 19,638 tonnes, accommodating 375 passenger cars and 1,500 passengers. Other examples of these super-size catamarans are found in the Brittany Ferries fleet with the Normandie Express and the Normandie Vitesse.

Case Study Irish Ferries

The distinctive green and blue livery of Irish Ferries has come a long way since the early pioneering days of the 1970s. Today, their fleet of 'cruise ferries' is one of the most modern and luxurious at sea, and a vital aspect of the Irish economy and the tourist business on both sides of the Irish Sea.

Irish Ferries began their passenger and freight services between Ireland and France in 1973, as a joint venture between Irish Shipping, Fearnley & Eger and Swedish company Lion Ferry, under the banner of Irish Continental Line (ICL). The new company opened a link between Rosslare, some 100 miles south of Dublin, with the *Saint Patrick*.

When Irish Shipping went into liquidation in 1984, Irish Continental Line was sold off in a management buyout and emerged as Irish Continental Group. The Irish–French route developed over the next decade, with larger tonnage, as more Irish and French tourists wanted to take their car abroad. Eventually the service boasted two ships on the Le Havre and Cherbourg links: The *Saint Killian II* and *Saint Patrick II*.

In 1992, ICG took over the British and Irish Steam Packet Company Limited, a nationalised company known as B&I (which traded under the name B + I Line) and which operated ferry services between Dublin and Holyhead and between Rosslare and Pembroke Dock. As part of its offer to buy B&I, management at ICG undertook to invest in replacing what was an ageing fleet. Over the following decade, a programme of fleet renewal was undertaken involving investment of €500 million.

In 1995 the first purpose-built ferry for the company, the *Isle of Innisfree*, entered service between Dublin and Holyhead. This was the start of a literary theme subsequently carried throughout the fleet, utilising a W.B. Yeats poem title: the vessel being named and launched by Clodagh Moreland, the wife of ICG CEO Eamonn

HONFLEUR ARRIVING AT CAEN

Artist's impression taken from builder's plans. Courtesy Mason Shipbrokers Ltd., London

SEATRUCK POWER ON THE RIVER MERSEY

30x40 inches. Oil on canvas. Courtesy Seatruck

Rothwell. The *Isle of Innisfree* was quickly followed by a larger sister ship, the Isle of Inishmore, which could carry some 2,200 passengers and 850 cars.

The continued growth of traffic between Ireland and the UK saw the introduction in 2001 of the *Ulysses*.

The new ferry was named after what is arguably the most important novel of the modernist movement, *Ulysses*, written by the Irish writer James Joyce. Set during one day in Dublin, the controversial stream-of-consciousness novel roughly parallels

Homer's Odyssey, albeit through the eyes of early twentieth century Ireland. Joyce, who was brought up in Dublin, became a short story writer and poet as well as a novelist, writing recognisable titles such as Dubliners and Finnegan's Wake. Despite sailing away from Dublin as a young man, he always returned to the city in his writing. With Joyce regarded as one of the most influential and important authors of the 20th century, and with strong links to Dublin, it's fitting that the great ferry was named *Ulysses*.

W.B. YEATS INWARD BOUND TO DUBLIN
Pictured passing the Poolbeg Light. 30x40 inches. Oil on canvas. Courtesy of Irish Ferries

ISLE OF INISHMORE
Pictured outward bound from Dublin. 20x30 inches. Watercolour. Courtesy Irish Ferries

ULYSSES PASSING HOWTH
20x30 inches. Watercolour. Courtesy Irish Ferries

OSCAR WILDE PASSING THE TUSKAR LIGHTHOUSE
25x35 inches. Oil on canvas. Courtesy Irish Ferries

W.B YEATS
Pictured passing Howth Head outward bound to Holyhead.
30x40 inches. Oil on canvas. Courtesy Irish Ferries

At the time of her introduction *Ulysses* was the world's largest car ferry in terms of lane meters / car-carrying capacity. She stands some 12 decks high, towering over most other ferries at a height of 51 metres from keel to mast. The Ulysses has five vehicle decks, which can carry overall some 1,340 cars or 241 articulated trucks and trailers (or a mix of cars and freight vehicles). Her extensive passenger accommodation is located over three decks, which include a Club Class lounge with magnificent sea views, a cinema, two bars, brasserie, cafe, a wide range of cabins, an exclusive freight drivers' area and a large shop and fashion boutique.

Following the introduction of the *Ulysses*, the *Isle of Inishmore* was transferred to the Rosslare–Pembroke Dock link to expand and improve operations.

In July 1999, Irish Ferries introduced a fast ferry service between Dublin and Holyhead. The new craft, the *Jonathan Swift*, increased the passenger capacity on the Dublin–Holyhead route by 73% and car capacity by 50%. The new operation allowed passengers to cross the Irish Sea in just under two hours. The *Jonathan Swift* was designed to allow quick turnarounds at port and was also designed with a bow door to allow vehicles to drive on at either end and drive straight off at port. In 2018 she was replaced by a larger craft, the *Dublin Swift*. This new addition to the Irish Ferries fleet is now the largest on the Irish Sea, and now the only fast ferry operation on the Irish Sea between Ireland and the UK.

As part of further investment in their operations the company acquired a new ship for their Irish/French link in 2007 to replace the *Normandy*. Following an extensive refit for her new role, the ship emerged as the *Oscar Wilde,* significantly improving the quality and standard of operations.

Five years later, further tonnage was introduced with the *Epsilon*, chartered for the Dublin–Holyhead route and for additional capacity at weekends on a new link from Dublin to Cherbourg. The new operation to France from the capital was later to be the key to Irish Ferries' decision to operate all their Irish / French services from Dublin, commencing 2019, with their new ship the *W.B.Yeats*.

In September 2017, the keel section of the new €144 million cruise ferry was laid. The new ship would have space for 1,885 passengers and crew, 440 cabins (including luxury suites with their own private balconies), and almost 3 km of freight deck lane meters, plus a dedicated car deck for 296 cars separate to this. Other facilities would include a Club Class lounge with direct passenger access from the car decks, á la carte and self-service restaurants, a cinema, shopping mall, choice of bars and lounges, exclusive areas for freight drivers, and dedicated facilities for pets. The ship was later named *W.B.Yeats*, after one of the greatest poets of the 20th century and one of Ireland's foremost literary figures.

William Butler Yeats was born in Dublin and educated in both Ireland and London. The decision by Irish Ferries to name their new vessel *W.B.Yeats* continues the tradition adopted by the company of selecting names drawn from the world of Irish literature. Recipient of a Nobel Prize for Literature in 1923, Yeats helped to found Dublin's famous Abbey Theatre, which opened in December 1904, incidentally the year in which Joyce's Ulysses is set.

He was born in Sandymount, County Dublin, in 1865, his family relocated to England in 1867, but returned to Dublin in 1880, where Yeats resumed his education. Through his family's artistic endeavours, the young man was surrounded by artists and writers, and it is through these connections that he seems to have taken to poetry, with the Dublin University Review publishing his first poems in 1885. Among the poems for which he is most fondly remembered is 'The Lake Isle of Innisfree', a composition inspired by his many holiday visits to Sligo, where, in a churchyard beneath Ben Bulben, his remains now rest.

On 19th January 2018, the completed hull of the new Irish Ferries cruise ferry, *W.B.Yeats*, was ceremonially named and launched by Rikki Rothwell, daughter of Eamonn Rothwell, CEO and Executive Director of Irish Continental Group. Commenting at the launch, Andrew Sheen, Managing Director said:

'The launch of our new cruise ferry *W.B.Yeats* – and the expectation of our second new cruise ferry, yet to come – herald in a new era in ferry travel between Ireland, the UK and Continental Europe bringing with its new standards in terms of passenger and freight capacity, comfort and reliability beyond anything previously envisaged'.

The *W.B.Yeats* arrived from the builders prior to Christmas. Following crew training she initially entered service between Dublin and Holyhead. As from March 2019, she will offer up to four sailings a week directly from Dublin to France; the flagship cruise ferry will travel 125,000 nautical miles per annum in her new role, which is the equivalent of circumnavigating the globe nearly six times. Irish Ferries will be the only operator providing customers with a direct crossing from Dublin direct to France.

The *W.B.Yeats* offers superior comfort to 1,800 passengers with 440 spacious cabins, including luxury suites with stunning private balcony sea views and a dedicated cabin steward service. Styled throughout in natural tones, rich furnishings are accented by marble, steel and state-of-the-art lighting, creating a relaxed and contemporary atmosphere on every deck. Décor in the passenger areas exudes understated elegance, illustrated by famous works of art and literature from Yeats and other well-known artists, while downloadable audio extracts from the famous poet's celebrated catalogue provide the backdrop to a unique walking tour.

From refined accommodation to fine dining, the literary theme continues throughout the ship. Guests are invited to indulge in innovative cuisine in the Lady Gregory Restaurant, enjoy a casual snack in the Maud Gonne Bar & Lounge or immerse themselves in the magic of movies and family fun entertainment at The Abbey and The Peacock cinemas.

Speaking ahead of the arrival, Andrew Sheen, said: 'We're delighted to bring the *W.B.Yeats* and its superior luxury to Dublin. The introduction of this magnificent new ship offers holidaymakers unrivalled comfort, with direct route access from the convenient and centrally located Dublin Port to France. Irish Ferries look forward to welcoming passengers onboard the *W.B.Yeats* to sail in style in 2019.'

In addition, the company plan to commence building a second, even larger cruise ferry for delivery in 2020. The new giant ferry is intended for service on the Dublin–Holyhead route. This second new vessel will be the largest cruise ferry in the world in terms of vehicle capacity, with accommodation for 1,800 passengers and crew. Her vehicle decks will have 5,610 freight lane metres, providing the capability to carry 330 freight units per sailing – a 50% increase in peak freight capacity compared to the current vessel, *Ulysses*.

Today, Irish Ferries carry over 1.5m passengers, 392,000 cars and 283,700 trucks to Ireland from Britain and France, with one of the most modern fleet of five ships in northern Europe.

Robert Lloyd has produced a wide selection of paintings for the company over the years following the introduction of the *Isle of Innisfree*. The featured ships are mostly set around the historical port of Dublin. Many of his commissioned paintings hang in their offices in Dublin, a sure tribute to their success and to the pioneering era of the new tonnage they have introduced during the 21st century on the Irish Sea.

SAILING SHIPS, NAVAL SHIPS, YACHTS AND SPECIAL COMMISSIONS

THE SUPERYACHT TALITHA G ANCHORED OFF EAST COWES DURING COWES WEEK, 2005

The 262.47ft motor yacht 'Talitha G' was built by Krupp Germaniawerft in Germany at their Kiel shipyard, she was delivered to her owners in 1929 and last refitted in 2008 by Devonport Yachts. Bannenberg & Rowell is responsible for her beautiful exterior and interior design. Previously named Reveller, Her interior configuration has been designed to comfortably accommodate up to twelve guests overnight in 6 cabins, comprising a master suite, 2 double cabins and 3 twin cabins. She is also capable of carrying up to eighteen crew onboard to ensure a relaxed luxury yacht experience. 30x40 inches. Oil on canvas. Courtesy Getty Estate

THE CLASSIC MOTOR YACHT NERO

Pictured off the northern coast of Mallorca. 20x30 inches. Oil on canvas. Private collection

GIORGIA

The motor yacht is pictured under way off the Island of Capri.
25x35 inches. Oil on canvas. Courtesy Nigel and Sue Pritchard

THE SAILING YACHT SEAHORN

Pictured off the Island of Stromboli.
25x35 inches. Oil on canvas. Courtesy Michael Aiken

HMS AGAMEMNON AT THE BATTLE OF DARDANELLES IN 1917
20x30 inches. Oil on canvas. Courtesy David Kenwright.

THE RRS DISCOVERY
Pictured in the Antarctic in 1903. 25x35 inches. Private collection

HMS AGAMEMNON
*Pictured at the battle of Genoa in 1795, firing a broadside at the French ship **Ca Ira**.*
25x35 inches. Oil on canvas. Courtesy David Kenwright

THE MARY ROSE

30x40 inches. Oil on canvas. Courtesy Michael Aiken

ACKNOWLEDGEMENTS

I would like to sincerely thank all those individuals, companies and organisations who have, over the years entrusted me with creating the paintings contained within this book.

My grateful thanks to Captain Kevin Oprey for his generous and charming introduction and for his wonderfully evocative description of the painting In Deep Water. To Jeff Macklin not only for his paintings of 'Miami Ships' but also his personal recollections and research which bring the paintings to life. To Chi Chien Hsu, one of my longest standing customers, a font of maritime knowledge and a shipowner with a real interest not only in his family's rich maritime history but in shipping in general.

A special thanks to David Kenwright, as close to a modern-day patron as it is possible to get. Jack Fahy and Frank Trumbour, two people who not only appreciate what I do but love ships the way they used to be.

As always, a book of this type is only possible because people want paintings, to Neda Maritime, the ever-supportive Michael Lykiardopulo and Karen Grout, to Jack Hsu of Oak Maritime, Qatargas, ExxonMobil, Ardmore Shipping, Cunard Line Angus Struthers, Carnival Corporation, Alistair Eagles at Seatruck. Damen Shipyard Group, Vincent Amabile, Thome Shipmanagement, Navigator Gas, Seabourn Cruises, Ed Carr at MOL LNG, Teekay Corporation, Irish Ferries, Offshore Shipbrokers Ltd, Des Kirkpatrick, Mike Aiken, Viking Cruises, Uniworld Boutique Cruises, RasGas, Michael Gallagher Rob Grool for his beautiful 'seas' with no ships and those 'with' ships. To Des and Ulla Cox who helped get me started. Charles Cen, Wan Hai Lines and Captain Ian Tew, the American Bureau of Shipping, The International Maritime Organisation, Efthimios Mitropoulos and Ionic Shipmanagement. To all at GulfMark Offshore, in one way or another my longest standing customers and deserving of a special place in this book. To all those private individuals who have helped me along the way, kept a roof over my head and entrusted me with a painting (or two).

None of these images would be included if it were not for Colin Fanning, a brilliant photographer and customers wouldn't be happy if it were not for the perfect framing by Paul Jacobs at Wisteria Gallery.

Special thanks of course to Miles Cowsill and his team at Lily Publications for agreeing to do another book – it looks wonderful.

Lastly and arguably most importantly, to my ever-enduring wife Victoria and my two daughters, Emilia and Lily – sorry for the late nights.